Contents

What is pottery?

Introduction

The basic principle in the making of clay pots has not changed since they were first made in Neolithic times over 20,000 years ago. Clay is now, as then, shaped, dried, and burned to make it permanent. Neanderthal man of the ice ages had been a hunter and made no pots, the ready-made shell and gourd being all he needed. But he knew about clay and its fire-change into stone – magic or the beginning of science? – and from the four elements, earth and water, fire and air, he made a ritual doll, or fertility goddess. Pots were first made thousands of years later, when climatic changes brought about revolutionary ways of providing food, through farming.

Since those crude beginnings, the story of pottery has simply been the continual discovery of additional natural materials and the improvement in methods of making. The primitive potter worked slowly by hand, taking many minutes or hours to shape pots which today are made in moments with machines. Where he polished, scratched or incised to decorate the surface, now there are many possible variations of colour, texture and glaze from which to choose. Firing has changed from a laborious and haphazard procedure to the mere pressing of a switch and fairly predictable results. Yet the basic process is still clay, shaped, dried and burned.

Today, pottery is one of a group of techniques under the general heading of 'ceramics', a term derived from *kerameikos*, the Greek word for both the material and the work of the potter. Ceramics are now defined as man-made articles, shaped from natural earths, rocks and minerals, and transformed into a permanent hard state by heat. Besides pots for everyday use in the home, the term includes a wide range of articles used in building, industry and science – bricks and tiles, pipes and sanitary ware, insulators and retorts, abrasives and furnace linings.

Each age leaves behind not only its everyday pots, but also man's everyday thoughts, made permanent as magical objects, decorative, ritual or aesthetic. And such is the versatility and richness of ceramic materials that creative man still finds through them a means for the imaginative expression not only of his most sophisticated whims, but also his most profound and solemn feelings.

The basic process

In the production of any ceramic article there are at least two stages, but generally three: (a) the shaping, (b) the first firing, called the *biscuit*, and (c) the second firing, called the *glost*.

By applying the glaze to the unfired or raw pot, the biscuit firing can be combined with the glost. This is obviously an economic advantage but, apart from difficulties of handling, there are limitations and disadvantages.

Decorative treatment can be applied between each stage, and after the glost firing, when a third firing becomes necessary.

The materials

There are four groups of ceramic materials: (a) the clay or plastic earths, (b) the fusible or non-plastic earths, (c) the fluxes, and (d) the ceramic colours.

Clay

Clay is a bodymaker, the one material essential for all ceramic processes. It can be defined as a natural fine-grained earth which develops plasticity when mixed with water. As one of the most

Step-by-Step Guide to
Pottery

GWILYM THOMAS

HAMLYN

London · New York · Sydney · Toronto

Acknowledgements

My thanks to the family brains-pool (two scientists and three artists), who helped me get this book right.

My thanks also to the following people, who kindly lent their work to illustrate it: pupils of the Northfleet School for Boys in Kent; Charmian Barker, Phyllis Blackall, Zel Ferridge, Maureen Morris and Jean Woods, all students of the Adult Centre, Maidstone, Kent; Elizabeth Davies, a student at the Sidcup Arts Centre, Kent; Rachel Thomas, a student at the Manchester Polytechnic; Elizbeth Kark, a student at the Hammersmith College of Art and Building; and Margaret Kissack and Sheila Rusby, both practising artists. Initials in the caption text acknowledge the pieces individually.

The photographs were taken specially for this book by Hawkley Studio Associates. The line drawings were done by Ron Hayward.

Published by
The Hamlyn Publishing Group Limited
London · New York · Sydney · Toronto
Astronaut House, Feltham, Middlesex, England

© Copyright The Hamlyn Publishing Group Limited 1973
Revised edition 1982

ISBN 0 600 34297 2

Printed in England

common deposits on the face of the earth, it is not surprising that clay's plastic qualities were soon discovered or that its transmutation by heat was noticed, perhaps under a continual fire. Pottery, then, probably did not evolve in one place. And throughout history potters have been aware of the differences in clays: in degrees of plasticity; in variations of colour after firing and strengths at different temperatures; and in suitability for making plant pots or teacups, terracotta figures or insulators.

The plasticity of clay is explained by the shape of its smallest particle. Under a powerful microscope, this is seen to be a very thin and flake-like crystal, usually elongated and six-sided. Because it is so thin each flake, with the right amount of water, clings and slides on the next, forming a strong bond, like two sheets of glass. A mass of flakes can be squeezed a great deal without breaking or collapsing and will retain its shape indefinitely, especially when allowed to dry and become hard. Dry clay-tiles used by the Egyptians for keeping records have been found intact after thousands of years. Too much water in the mixture would loosen the bond, making the mass soft and weak, too little having the opposite effect. This water of plasticity is 'free': it dries out at normal temperatures. Dry clay needs only to absorb water to become plastic again.

The transmutation from clay to pot by heat is due to a change in the chemical and physical composition of the crystal, which is made up of three molecular compounds: alumina, silica, and water. This molecular water is eliminated when the clay is heated over 500°C, the crystal structure changes, and the clay becomes a hard permanent mass. Pot or biscuit, as it is then called, cannot be made plastic again however finely it may be ground. For practical purposes clays must be fired well above the point of dehydration. At 900°C a soft useable porous biscuit is produced, typical of most primitive pottery. It is still porous at 1100°C, the average temperature for earthenware, but it is now hard and strong.

At higher temperatures further changes take place, mainly the fusing of less resistant substances and a closer bonding together of all constituents. As a result, the body becomes dense and vitrified and now ceases to be porous. At still higher temperatures, further fusing can cause complete collapse. Impurities are the main contributory factors to the lack of resistance to heat. Common surface clays containing iron and calcium compounds are for this reason suitable only for low-temperature pottery.

In the firing of clay, water naturally changes into steam, expanding considerably. If this is forced by too rapid a rise in temperature, the effect is literally explosive, bursting the clay apart. Therefore not only must the water of plasticity be thoroughly dried out before firing, but the rise in temperature up to and beyond the point of dehydration must be controlled. Thick sections of clay will need a slower rise than thin ones.

Clays shrink both in drying and in firing, some more than others. This factor more perhaps than any other will cause faults, if not properly understood and allowed for. Faults will most usually appear during the drying stages; but if they do not reveal themselves before firing, they will afterwards. Shrinkage is due to the particles growing closer together and more compact as the water is removed by evaporation and dehydration. Where clays vary, they are not suitable for joining together. Uneven drying means uneven shrinkage, resulting in warping or cracking, especially in flat and shallow shapes, which are structurally weak. Plastic clay will not remain attached to dry clay since it alone will continue to shrink, and clay parts in different stages of drying will distort and crack or part at the joins. Uniform drying of all the parts of a composite work is imperative; the softer they are in the assembling, the better they will adjust to each other in the drying out, and the more sure the joins.

The shrinkage and plasticity of clay is reduced by the presence of sand. Fired clay, crushed to a powder called grog, can be used for the same purpose, eliminating the tendency of thin flat shapes to warp or of thick ones to burst. Grog is made from any unglazed fired ware, including broken

Playing cards illustrating the arrangement of clay crystals: how they lie and cling together to give plasticity. They are usually six sided and considerably thinner than these cards.

kiln furniture which being refractory adds this quality as well. Sand and grog also add coarse textures to clay bodies. Before use, they should be thoroughly washed to remove any scummy impurities, which cause bloating in firing.

Clay in its liquid state is called a slip, and it can be used in various colours to cover a clay body. Slip should fit, that is it should have the same shrinkage as the body, otherwise it will crack or flake off, after firing if not before. Fairly thin clay slip can be safely painted onto dry clay, whereas thick slip will peel off or crack dry pots if applied too quickly.

For the making of work of a precise finished size, the exact shrinkage in drying and in firing must be ascertained. This is done by comparing the measurements of a piece of clay before and after firing to the required temperature.

When first dug, clays are much too fresh and not ready for immediate use. The clay crystals are locked in bundles making the body 'short' or not as plastic as it might be. Weathering, or exposure to rain and frost through a winter, breaks up the clay and improves it. All manipulation of clay has a similar effect and this makes preparation an important process.

Nowadays, although natural deposits of clays suitable for all uses are available, bodies are also processed by potters' merchants in standardized mixtures for specific purposes. Local deposits are worth investigating if only as additions to prepared bodies, providing texture and colour, or as ingredients in glazes.

Clay can be classified into four main groups: red clays, ball clays, china clays and fireclays.

Red clays are the most commonly found in deposits on or near the surface of the earth. Geologists call them secondary clays because they have been eroded and carried from their primary source by natural agents, frost, rain, and river, to become huge sedimentary deposits at the bottom of lakes and seas. As they are borne along, these clays come into contact with other natural substances, such as sand, calcium and iron compounds. Iron, for instance, colours them red or yellow, and some clays are blue or green grey with organic matter but burn out to red. Various impurities lower the clays' resistance to heat, making them suitable only for earthenwares.

Ball clays are also secondary deposits, but free of impurities. They burn almost white, especially a variety black with organic matter, and, having a greater resistance to heat, are used for stoneware and porcelain bodies. They can be too plastic to be used alone, high shrinkage tending to cause warping and cracking. This is remedied by adding less plastic clays or non-plastic materials such as sand or grog.

China clay is a primary deposit, found where it was formed – by the decomposition of granite rocks. It is the purest form of clay, white-burning, refractory, and almost non-plastic; for these reasons, it is valuable for blending with ball clays in stoneware and porcelain bodies, and as a source of pure alumina in glazes.

Fireclays are secondary clays found under coal seams, having been deposited in swampy forests. They are highly resistant to heat, being siliceous and free of impurities, and therefore valuable for making furnace bricks and other refractories. They are coarse, but plastic when finely ground. They open finer and more plastic bodies, adding texture and strength, and in reducing atmospheres (see page 49) the trace of iron they contain makes a black speckle.

Fusible earths

The second group of ceramic materials are the glaze formers. They are feldspars, Cornish stones, and silicas in the form of flint, quartz, and sand. These earths tend to fuse at a high temperature, but one which is too high for practical purposes. By the addition of fluxes (see below), this melting point can be lowered to produce a glassy melt or glaze.

A glaze requires three components: a fluxing oxide, alumina (aluminium oxide), and silica (silicon oxide). Cornish stones and feldspars contain alumina, silica, and varying amounts of flux; unadulterated clays contain alumina and silica; flint, quartz and white sand are pure forms of silica; and china clay is pure alumina: these and other raw materials which contain one or another glaze ingredient can be used in combination with fluxes to form a glaze.

Fusible earths can also be used in the making of bodies to give specific qualities: Cornish stone and feldspar help to vitrify stoneware and porcelain bodies.

Fluxes

These are materials added to the glaze formers to lower their melting point to a required temperature. They occur naturally in fusible earths, but are added in the form of oxides and carbonates, and also as *frits*, which are pre-melted fluxes. The main fluxes are lead, sodium, and calcium, others being potassium, boron, magnesium, lithium, and barium.

Lead compounds, soda and borax are low-temperature fluxes. They are used as frits for raku and earthenware glazes, melted with another glaze ingredient, usually silica, in the case of lead to eliminate its effect as a poison, and in the others to make them insoluble in water. Glaze materials must be insoluble in water, that is in suspension, so that the glaze will remain a consistent mixture when it dries on the biscuit. A soluble ingredient would separate out from the others as the water evaporated.

Soda is also used in salt glazing on stoneware, common salt (sodium chloride) being made to volatilize from the firemouth into the kiln chamber at maximum temperature. It combines with the clay surface to form a glaze.

Calcium, in the form of whiting, is the usual flux at high temperatures, and vegetable ashes provide an insoluble form of potassium and calcium. Lithium, barium, and magnesium are used for colour variation.

Ceramic colours

Metallic compounds are the basis of all ceramic colours, vegetable and other organic sources having no resistance to heat.

Iron is the most common and most versatile of all, used mostly as red iron oxide, but also as yellow, purple and magnetic oxides and crocus martis. In earthenwares it makes rich honey yellows and browns and near black. In stoneware its range extends to variations of jade greens and blues (celadon), purple red browns and blacks (tenmoku), olive greens and browns, and yellows and orange when used with titanium.

Copper is green under most conditions in earthenware and stoneware, turns blood red in high-temperature reduction, and black and metallic when thickly applied but then inclined to fuse and run. It changes from an emerald green with lead and calcium as fluxes to turquoise blues with soda, borax, lithium, and barium. It tends to spread and fog at the edges, penetrate clay, and even jump the space between pots.

Cobalt is a stable blue under most conditions and temperatures, but it turns pink if isolated from alumina. It is the strongest staining oxide and needs to be used sparingly.

Manganese produces purple browns and maroons and is useful for blacks in combination with iron and cobalt.

Antimony produces yellows, but is stable only in earthenware.

Uranium is stable for yellows in stoneware.

Chrome generally fires a smoky yellow green, but it makes pink with tin in earthenware. Like copper it fogs at the edges and spreads.

Tin, titanium, zinc and zircon are white opacifying oxides, tin the whitest, titanium a warm white. Zinc at high temperatures becomes a flux. Rutile is crude titanium with some iron and produces a broken effect with other colours.

These are the raw materials used in ceramics for making bodies, glazes, and colours, and a potter can use them to prepare his own. However, from them manufacturers make and supply a wide range of standard preparations, saving the craftsman much work.

Types of pottery

After 10,000 years of discovery, development and imaginative expression, it is not surprising that pottery has become extremely varied and complex. It can be classified in many ways – by the place or period in which it was made, by the material or process used, by the use to which it is put, or by its purely decorative qualities.

But the simplest and most basic division is into two main types – porous and non-porous. And the difference is due to the maximum temperature at which the pot is fired. Below 1150°C pots are, for the most part, porous. From 1200°C upwards they become vitrified or non-porous. Not all clays are suitable for vitrification, but all can be used at the lower temperatures.

Earthenwares are porous, usually red or brown, but also white. The maximum firing temperature ranges from as low as 700°C in raku firing to 1150°C or higher for really hard earthenware for domestic use; the average is 1100°C. Until the twelfth century, when porcelain was first brought to Europe from China, all pottery of the Mediterranean area, the Middle East and Europe was earthenware. In the main this continued to be so until almost the eighteenth century, when the making of stoneware and porcelain was finally understood in the West.

If they are to hold a liquid, porous pots must be glazed, and the glaze must not craze or crack; if it does, liquids will naturally seep through. Until the right glaze materials were found and understood, primitive potters sealed their pots with oils and resins. Glazes came into general use on earthenware in Europe with the spread of Islam from the Middle East, the opaque white tin glaze of the Islamic potters becoming known as maiolica in Spain and Italy, as delft and faience in Holland, France, and England. A clear lead glaze was used on slipware in England.

Stoneware and porcelain are vitrified, non-porous. Whereas stoneware is dense and opaque, porcelain is translucent. Although pottery began much later in the Far East, progress in the making of porcelain and stoneware outstripped the West by many centuries, reaching possibly the highest-ever technical standards by AD 900. Bone china and soft-paste porcelain are similar to porcelain, produced industrially at a lower and more economic temperature. Bone china is made in England, and is so called because calcined bone is used as the vitrifying ingredient in the body.

Preparation

Careful preparation of all ceramic materials is an absolute necessity, that of the clay body being first and most important of all. Like a musical instrument, clay should be in tune immediately before use. Mixing the clay, or *wedging*, puts life into it, and the more thorough the wedging the more plastic strength it gains. Properly wedged clay responds readily and dependably to the potter's touch.

Although potters' merchants now supply bodies in a plastic condition ready to use, and pug mills, or mechanical mixers, are commonly installed in the workshop for the recovery of waste material, it does not follow that wedging has been made unnecessary. On the contrary, it is still an essential preliminary to all processes with a plastic body; and it should moreover be a personal affair, when the potter becomes familiar with and close to his partner.

Wedging ensures two things: first a homogeneous consistency in the mass of the clay, and second the absence of air cavities. Clay which is uneven or lumpy will not respond or move smoothly, and pockets of air not only feel like hard lumps, but expand and bloat or burst in firing. If the clay is not clean in the first place, there could well be a third reason for wedging, the removal of rubbish. This can quite easily get into the clay, especially under conditions in a class workshop shared by many students. Bits of wood, cloth, wire, sponge, plaster, and paper left carelessly lying around can easily be picked up in the clay and have disastrous effects in the firing. During the process of wedging, they can be detected, removed, and properly disposed of, not left on the bench. The wedging bench should be clean, free even from dry clay, which will not soften in the mixture, also from sand or grog, which, although not harmful, are a nuisance in random amounts.

And, of course, it should be left clean after use.

Wedging is done by a continual process of folding the clay, by kneading and by dividing the lump in two by hand or with a wire and slamming the halves together. It is best to do the latter first, so as to cut up any stiff parts and enable a clear examination of the section, judging its condition and progress. This continuous doubling of the lump results in a laminated formation like the leaves of a book, but the individual 'leaves' become progressively thinner until they disappear in an absolutely even mix. It should be pointed out that this lamination is consistent with the crystal structure of clay, giving the mass cohesive and plastic strength as the crystal flakes are made to lie more closely and compactly together.

Hand kneading in smaller lumps follows to complete the work. However, when the clay is known to be clean and free of stiff lumps, kneading alone will be enough. The softness of the clay is a matter for individual choice, according to the process or work in hand.

The next step, dividing the clay, depends on what is to be made. If only an occasional piece is required for modelling or coiling, it should be removed from the main lump as the work proceeds, taking the precaution of keeping the prepared clay covered to prevent drying out. Pieces should not be carelessly clawed off, making air cavities, especially when the whole lump is to be divided into weighed pieces for repetition throwing.

Wedging

1 **Cutting and slapping in the hand**
The clay lump is flattened and held edge-wise in the cupped left hand, the thumb being horizontal and halfway up the lump. The right hand takes the upper half, the right thumb opposite and just above the left, ready to push through, not twist, the lump. The hands should be relaxed, not gripping the clay or clawing it with the fingers.

2 The right thumb is pushed through the lump; cutting it against the horizontal left thumb with an action like a pair of scissors or the tearing in half of a book.

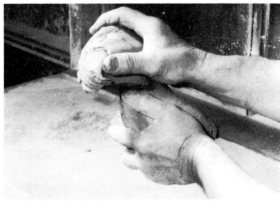

3 Slamming the two parts together. With a slight shift of the piece in the right hand, it is lined up to match the other piece so that the torn faces lie side by side as the right hand brings its half down on the other.

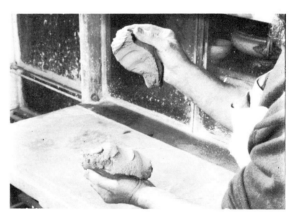

4 The slamming and doubling completed. The hands are relaxed and flat, the fingers together, not clawing and digging into the clay and causing cavities, and the whole lump has been slightly flattened by the slam. Next it is turned at right angles in the left hand and held as in step 1, the torn edges upwards, and the cutting is repeated. The doubling results in an increasing layering of the lump.

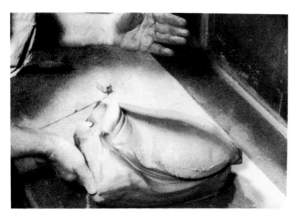

Cutting and slapping on the bench

1 This is a process similar to hand wedging, but used for much larger lumps of clay cut with a wire. The bench should be heavy and solid, with an unpolished top, and kept continually clean with a scraper so that the clay does not stick. The lump is first flattened and then dropped flatwise at a slope, the further edge resting on the bench and the near edge raised.

2 A wire held taut between the hands is passed halfway under the lump and raised vertically through it to cut it in two. Both sections should be examined for pieces of rubbish or extra-hard lumps of clay. Rubbish should be properly disposed of, not left on the bench. Hard lumps can be put in the waste-bin or hand-mixed with soft clay and returned to the main lump. The wire may need wiping to remove any stranded rubbish it has dragged out.

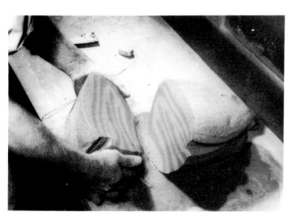

3 After cutting with the wire, the nearer half of the lump should fall freely away from the other half. When the sections have been examined and passed, the free half is picked up with a hand on each side and turned so that its section is facing the same way as the other one.

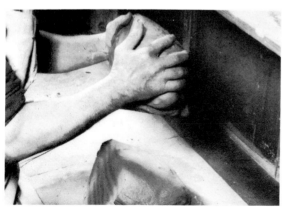

4 The free half is lifted well above the other and slammed down to double the lump and produce the first two layers. In slamming, the hands should stay on the clay, its weight being used to do the work: more energy is used in releasing and throwing the lump down, and the aim is often less accurate.

5 So far there have been three actions— dropping, cutting, and slamming—and now there is a fourth before repeating the sequence. This consists simply of making the upper surface of the lump a little flatter and neater. First the lump is pulled forward off the bench, a hand on each side, and then …

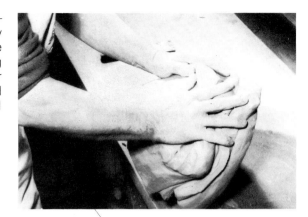

6 … it is turned completely over to flatten what was the upper face. To start the sequence again and repeat the wedging, the lump is pulled forward once more and turned 90° before being dropped sloping on the bench ready for the next cut. This turn means that each succeeding cut is at right angles to the one before. The dotted line drawn on the lump indicates the direction of the cut made in step 2.

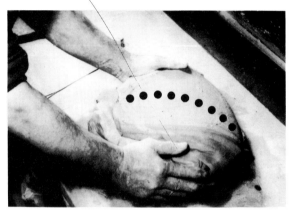

7 The laminated formation in the clay lump resulting from the continual folding action of cutting and slamming, here demonstrated with bodies of different colours.

8 The effect of lamination on air cavities can be clearly demonstrated if holes are deliberately poked down into the lump. After only two cuts and slams this is the result: the deep holes have become flattened cavities between the layers of clay and in spreading have been quickly cut through by the wire. With continual cutting and slamming all the air will be forced out and the layering will disappear in a homogeneous mixture.

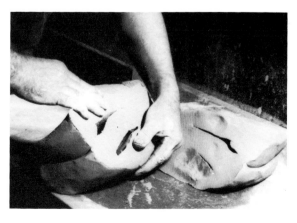

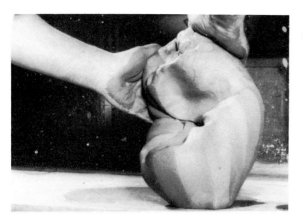

Kneading round

1 The action is a continuous turning and folding into the middle of the lump, producing a shape like a sea shell. This is the first position, the top of the stroke, shown with the 'shell' on its point. In this case the actual folding is done with the right hand, the left simply supporting and holding the lump as the right hand moves round. The thrust is downwards with the heel of the hand …

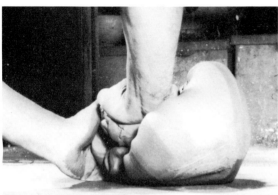

2 … to the bottom of the stroke and the top is folded into the middle. The whole movement follows through in a smooth and continuous rolling action …

3 … forward and round …

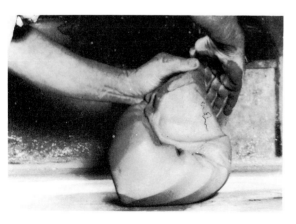

4 … and up onto the point of the shell-shaped lump in a complete circle, the left hand carrying the lump round while the right hand moves further on to a fresh position for the next thrust into the centre. The whole body must be relaxed, weight coming down from the shoulders through the straight right arm. The bench height should allow the feet to be placed well apart, with the arm straight and the heel of the hand just resting on the bench.

Kneading forward

1 This is another way of folding the clay, but with a forward-only action. The lump is pulled up on its edge and the heels of the hands fold the clay downwards and forwards into the mass.

2 As the action follows through, the clay is rolled forwards, becoming cylindrical with a nose-like lump growing between the two hands and giving the whole mass the appearance of a bull face. The elongated lump must be turned frequently, rolled together, and the kneading repeated.

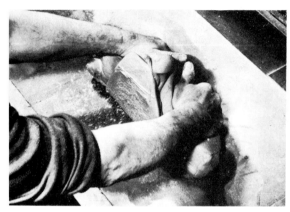

Weighing and balling up

After wedging, the whole lump is shaped into a rectangular block and placed on end. It is then quartered and cut horizontally into cubes with a wire. With practice a fairly accurate weight can be cut. The pieces, having been neatly rounded and stacked on a bat, are covered with a damp cloth or plastic sheet ready for use on the wheel.

Mixing by chopping

A method of mixing small batches of grogged or coloured bodies, or waste material, when a pug mill is either not available or not to be contaminated. It is done on a wooden bench by chopping with a flat metal bar. The clay splays open in overlapping layers, which are chopped again and again. Water or slurry is added if necessary to soften the clay. At intervals the clay is stacked and chopping continued. It is followed by wedging.

Making methods

Introduction

The behaviour of soft clay in the hand is direct and immediate, spontaneous and intriguing, its response arousing visual and tactile excitement. To roll out a strip or ball, pinch up rigid points, slap out a slice or penetrate with a stiff finger comes naturally to the human hand.

And the hand was the original pivot in the turning principle basic to wheel-making processes. The modern industrial machine uses this principle in exactly the same way as a pair of Neolithic hands once did. The ball of clay is rounded, centred, penetrated, opened and drawn up spirally from the turning centre. The difference is that of pace and shows in the character of the finished article, irregular and uneven from the hands, cold and precise from the machine, springing fluidly from the throwing wheel.

Pinching

The most straightforward making technique in pottery is the pinched- or thumb-pot method. Coming as it does from the cupped hand, the pinched pot naturally has a lip which undulates and a base which is rounded. This shape rests easily on soil, grass, sand, or hot embers. Size is limited by the capacity of the hand to cups and small bowls and composite pieces built up from these. Time is needed during the shaping to allow the soft hollowed clay to stiffen, lip down, and another ball can be opened while this is happening. When leather-hard, more thinning out is possible until the pot is twice its original size or more.

All pottery skills look deceptively easy, none more so than this method of shaping a pot by pinching out and turning in the cupped hand. To acquire the skill and sensitivity for this technique requires both patience and practice to an extent not fully realised at first by students content with a few clumsy efforts. Often regarded as a first ten-finger exercise, its greater possibilities, as a continuing opportunity for a wide range of creative expression, should be realised and appreciated.

Moulding

The idea of moulding clay probably occurred in different ways to different groups of people. Some found that pebbles could serve as natural block moulds, pivoted in the hand or on the hollowed top of a wooden stake; in the latter instance, the pot was inverted over the pebble and planished and polished to a regular size and shape – with both hands free the lip could be extended with additional pieces of clay. Others probably found that a slice of clay slapped out between the hands could be pressed with a fist into a hand cupped hollow to make a mould or stroked smoothly into it with a thumb. Moulding may originally have been suggested by man's first ready-made dish, the shallow shell. The early potters may also have used other naturally formed moulds, such as dried-up hollows in mud and sand, or cylindrical pieces of wood around which clay could be wrapped.

The principle of moulding requires that the clay should become firm enough to be removed easily from the mould, without losing its shape. Trial and error should quickly establish whether any locking of clay and mould is preventing easy separation. Open dish shapes release easily providing there is no turn in at the lip; solid formers which taper must slide out at the wide end; solids and parallel-sided shapes are more easily removed if wrapped in newspaper before moulding begins.

Sand provides a ready-made, easy-to-handle and adaptable material for mould-making. The

Wrap-round box (MK); rolled soft-slab three-sided form (CB); pierced three-sided open slab form (JW); finger- and tool-patterned tile (PB); carved form, pressed-slice ashtray and (see page 18) three-footed form (GT); and rigid-construction boxes and tesserae (RT).

addition of clay binds it and makes it firmer and more permanent. Dry sand should be added to thick slip or slurry until a fairly stiff mixture is formed. This is then put in a bowl, shallow box or deep tray and patted into an open hollow, using a pebble wrapped in a thin cloth. Thin paper laid over the sand and patted will help in making an even surface and can remain when the mould is used. Clay slices are carefully laid in, smoothed and allowed to become firm before being removed. The sand and clay mixture can be used indefinitely for fresh moulds.

Plaster of Paris moulds are not only more permanent but can also be duplicated from each other. Moulds for pressed work can be hollow for working on the inside, or of the convex, mushroom-type for working on the outside. Specially-shaped solids can also be made for wrapping.

Hollow pressing has certain advantages over the other method. In the first place, inside pressing is better managed, and the dish can shrink easily and release itself. In the second, the all-important upper face of the dish is available from the very start for decoration, so, beginning with clay at its softest, all the various methods of decoration before biscuit firing are possible. With the mushroom type of mould, there is the risk of the slice tightening on the mould as it shrinks, and splitting if the shape is deep. Also, with clay treatment, although decoration can be applied to the slice before it is moulded, this may not be as appropriate as when decorating a three-dimensional form, and if decorated when removed from the mould, the dish is very fragile and needs careful handling.

With the use of a flat bench top, slices of clay may be made by spreading out with the hand or a roller, or by cutting with a wire using suitable guides to determine thickness. The bench top should be of an absorbent material, such as unpolished wood, otherwise the clay slice will stick. Paper or, better still, non-fluffy canvas will also prevent sticking and can be a help afterwards in carrying the slice to the mould.

Slip casting makes use of the absorbent quality of the dry plaster mould. Filled with casting slip, it absorbs water from the slip and a layer of clay forms on the inside surface of the mould. When this has grown thick enough, the remaining slip is removed. Then the lining of clay is allowed to dry and shrink, and finally it is removed from the mould. This process affords craftsmen the means for reproducing ceramic pieces in limited numbers, each piece being subject to considerable individual treatment.

Joining

Joining parts in composite forms and sticking on pieces must take place well before the clay becomes hard: the softer it is the better. Then it is easy and sure, allowing for further modelling of the shape, and pieces can be readily nipped together to make a safe join. When they are stiff, slip has to be used to make the parts stick. They need to fit well together, the contact surfaces being softened with pricking and wetting and then well brushed with a ready supply of thick slip. A bad fit with uneven contacts filled with slip will result in cavities and cracks forming as the slip dries and shrinks. It is also important that all the parts should have dried to the same extent, otherwise distortion is bound to happen in their final state, after if not before firing.

There is a tremendous opportunity in these simple methods of making pots for exploring all the different bodies, materials, colours and glazes available, and for discovering their qualities, limitations and potential for form and decorative treatment. Since relatively small quantities are used, there is little waste of preparation time or material involved, but considerable knowledge to be gained. Smooth and rough bodies can be used, as well as slips, oxides and glazes, in an almost unlimited number of combinations.

Simple pinched pot

1 This ball of fairly soft clay is about the size of the fist—it could be smaller or as large as the hand can manage. The lump must first be well rounded: any folds are likely to split in the pinching process. It is comfortably cupped in the left or right hand, and then penetrated with the thumb of the other as centrally as possible.

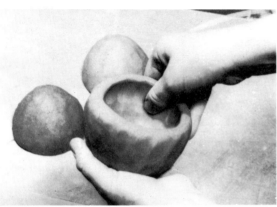

2 The opened ball is at first gently made even as it is turned in the cupped hand, and then starting at the bottom gradually pinched between the thumb on the inside and all the fingers on the outside, moving only the space of the thumb at a time. The clay may be turned either way as long as the whole surface is pinched in circles or spirally up to the lip. The more turning there is the more regular the shape is likely to be.

3 Several pieces should be made at a time because each needs to be pinched in at least two stages, allowing it to stiffen before trying to make the wall thinner. For this the piece is placed on its lip to dry evenly and to keep the rim regular. When the wall has been pinched out as thin as possible and the clay is stiff and firm, the whole shape is tidied, particular care being taken with the finishing of the lip.

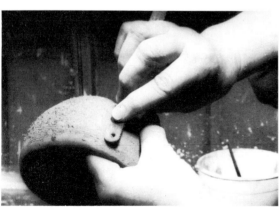

4 With the acquiring of skill through practice, there should be less and less need to clean up, the regularity and finish of the shape improving with the making. In the meantime various tools such as a hacksaw blade are useful for levelling off an uneven surface and at the same time adding various textures.

Composite pieces

1 Composite pieces are made by joining two or more pinched pots together. For a satisfactory union they should be in the same condition, and not firmer than leather hard. The contact edges, which should fit closely with both lips curving outwards slightly, are first roughened by light chopping with a knife, and then brushed with slip and firmly pressed together. Closing is done by running the thumb round the join.

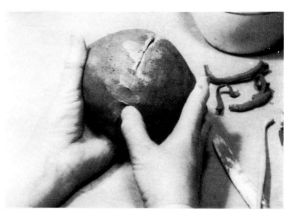

2 With a closed composite piece, one end can be opened and pinched into a mouth or neck and, if wished, extended into a bottle with a coil of clay. Through the opening, the inside of the join can be smoothed over and made sound.

Pinched pots are naturally rounded on the base and, unless they are tall, should stand well without tipping. A slight flattening at the base is enough to make shapes stable.

Examples

Mainly simple and composite pinched forms: birds shapes and marbled pot (SR); flower forms and large pierced pot (MK); grotesque animals (Northfleet); small pierced pot (MM); pebble (ZF); irregular pinched pot (GT). The exception is the hippo (ZF), which is thrown.

Slicing and soft construction

1 An old bucket handle with end loops can make a very simple tool for cutting slices of clay from a large lump. The loops are threaded with a taut wire, and sawcuts locate the wire as near the bottom of the loops as possible. Two strips of wood matched to the required thickness act as guides on which the wire is drawn through the clay. Each time a slice is cut the remaining lump is lifted to one side, and either the slice is removed or the process is begun again on another part of the bench.

2 Soft slices freely shaped according to the lump of clay as above can be assembled while still soft simply by nipping the edges together, slip being unnecessary. Working on a bat fixed to a banding wheel, or turntable, makes assembly and shaping easier and all-round viewing possible.

3 The assembly and further shaping of a three-sided slab form. The three sides have been nipped together and pinched out into fins, the bottom edges also being drawn together and three feet pinched out. The lip has been rounded, and the mouth is large enough for the handle of a screw driver to be inserted to belly out the pot still further. The clay is still soft from the lump and the interesting pattern of lines made by the wire remains on the slab sides, accentuating the fullness of the belly. Other simple slab forms are shown with various patterns impressed in the clay.

Another method of cutting clay into regular slices. Here the equipment is two pieces of hardwood slotted with sawcuts at measured intervals which can be threaded with wire. The sticks are held so as to make the wire taut and then drawn over the bench, cutting through the lump of clay. The wire is moved up into another pair of slots for the next cut, and so on. Thickness may vary but rolling can make the slices even. Interleaving with asbestolux bats dries the slices evenly and flat for tiles.

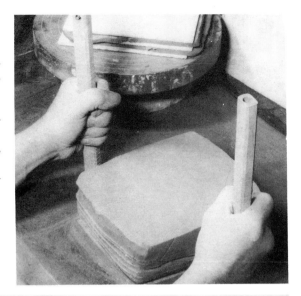

Moulds

A selection of moulds for pressing dishes and tiles. On the screw press is a wooden tile-mould faced with metal, consisting of frame, plain face-die, and keyed back-die. Slices of very stiff grogged body are cut to fit the mould; this is then pressed and the slices are pushed out with one of the dies. On the left are concave and convex moulds for the same plate shape (see page 21 for concave moulds), and centre front is the clay model of an oval dish on its plaster bat, plus the template and the metal strip for making the first mould, which is shown on the right (see page 62 for mould making).

Rolling out slices

1 Before using a roller to spread a lump of clay, it can be started with the hand or fist. To prevent the clay, which should not be too soft, from sticking to the bench, the work should be done on paper or, better still, a stiff smooth canvas. Reversing the slice at each rolling allows the clay to move easily on the canvas, a second piece being laid on top of extra large slices to make the tossing easier.

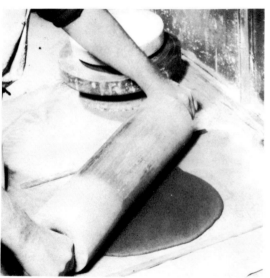

2 After the preliminary hand-batting, a wooden roller is used to produce an even slice. A pair of wooden strips on which the roller runs can be used to give an even thickness. However, with practice, guides become unnecessary and this gives the freedom to vary the thickness, making a slice taper towards the edge. With free rolling, the roller should be taken across at all angles, the edge being trimmed with a needle or thin knife to test the thickness; finally the edge is thinned to produce the taper.

3 Reversing the slice requires a sensitive grip, not too pinched or too near the edge. It should be peeled back, rather than lifted, from the canvas, which is conveniently held down by the roller. Larger thinner slices are lifted with the canvas, reversed onto another piece of canvas and the first one peeled off. Canvas can also be conveniently used to place a large slice on a mould.

Press moulding a dish

1 A small slice is being placed on a round dish-mould made of plaster of Paris. It should be gently laid in position, not dropped flat so that air is trapped between clay and mould. Observe the broad grip, well into the slice. The mould has been centred on a banding wheel and should be fixed either by three small nobs of clay at its edge (as here) or with a coil of clay pressed round it.

2 Then the slice is lightly pressed home all over and the overhanging waste edge is trimmed off. This should be cut with a fine needle or a wire, allowing at least half an inch spare over the edge of the mould. A knife is unsuitable for cutting soft clay because it drags. The banding wheel makes this trimming easy and quick. The wire should be held taut and as short as possible; if long, it could be caught up by the mould. In whichever direction the mould is turning, trimming should always be done on the side moving away.

3 Pressing into the mould. As always, thumb and finger are the best tools. At first the pressure should be light, using virtually the tip of the thumb, the clay being easily rucked up into lumps. This action is most effective with a spinning wheel because the slice can then be pressed in a series of rings or in a spiral. As the clay surface becomes firm, pressure can be increased to smooth out ridges, but it should be light at the lip to avoid making it thin and mean. Finally the spare clay is trimmed off close to the mould, taking care not to cut the plaster. The lip should be cut not obliquely thin but square, and then rounded off.

Wrap moulding

1 In this case the solid is a wooden block with parallel sides. It has been wrapped first in two pieces of newspaper, which were neatly trimmed and fitted at the base and held together with adhesive tape. The slice was freely rolled fairly thin and has an irregular shape.

2 The clay at the lower end of the block has been neatly trimmed of overlap and the edge of the slice brushed with slip to attach it to the slice on which it stands. This base is being trimmed with a thin-bladed knife. Notice how in wrapping the slice around the block it has been over-lapped, not trimmed to fit at any edge.

3 The clay was sufficiently soft for the over-lap to stick and now further batting is being applied. This not only regulates the shape and loosens the clay on the block, but also introduces a rhythmic pattern. Also shown are pieces with piercing and an overlap left as an irregular fin.

Box construction

1 A slice of clay has been carefully rolled out and is now being divided into precise shapes and sizes for a more rigid and exact piece of slab construction than was demonstrated on page 18. The slice has been allowed to stiffen considerably so that no distortion occurs in cutting with a thin-bladed knife. The accurate cutting needs a straight edge and a square so one edge of the slice is cut straight and a wooden strip is laid along it in order that the square can slide easily along and over the slice.

2 In planning rigid slab forms, it is necessary to be clear how the pieces fit together, allowing for their thickness. They can be cut exactly to a pattern, as a carpenter does with wood. Alternatively, with a simple box-shape, only the base and top need be cut accurately; four side pieces of the correct height are arranged so that they butt one against the other around the base; and after the top piece has been stuck in position the sides are trimmed at each corner. Here a wooden block is being used to check the corner as a side piece is attached. With fairly stiff clay slabs a perfect fit is essential to ensure good joins. Pieces to be joined must be equally stiff, and the contact edges are slipped and pressed thoroughly together.

3 To make a lid, the completed box is cut through near one end, using a square as a guide. This end section becomes the lid, thin strips of clay being attached inside it to form the lip. The illustration shows one such lid balanced on top of a box. The inside corners of boxes can be rounded off and strengthened with strips of waste clay, but they must be as stiff as the box otherwise they will shrink and crack. The outside corners can be made perfectly regular against a flat surface, by rolling or rubbing them, soft or hard.

Slip casting

1 A clay model being prepared for moulding. The simpler the model the easier the process, and the fewer the parts to the mould. This one has been divided into two with a flat clay strip about two inches wide which is well supported with clay to take the weight of plaster. A clay enclosing-wall is added round the bedding strip to retain the plaster while it sets, and a clay cone is attached at the mouth of the animal to form the 'spare' of the mould, through which it will be filled with slip. Buttons of clay are spaced on the clay bed to serve as keys, or 'natches', when fitting the two halves of the mould together. When the model is ready, plaster is mixed and, just before it begins to set, poured over the model to a depth of about two inches, the same as the clay bed. Details which protrude can be detached and moulded and cast separately to simplify the process. In this example the ears of the hippo have already been moulded.

2 Here the model is seen with both halves of the mould completed. When the first half has set hard, the whole job is turned over and the clay bed removed, leaving the model half bedded in plaster. Then the second half can be moulded in the same way as the first. Before this, however, the plaster face must be treated to prevent the second batch of plaster sticking to it. This is done by soap-washing the plaster face, creating a greasy surface to which fresh plaster will not stick. When the second part has set hard, the two halves can be separated as seen here, the function of the natches being clearly shown. The cylindrical spare piece has been removed.

3 Removing a cast from the mould. Before casting, the mould must be dried out, and this should not be forced by heat. Moulds can quite easily warp, and, unless tied together for drying, parts may be found not to fit later. For the casting, the bound mould is filled with slip until the spare is full, allowing for the level of the slip to drop as water is absorbed by the mould, and it should be kept topped up. Small moulds like the ears can be cast solid by pressing in plastic clay, waste from the casting being used. The thickness of the cast can be judged by the clay lining the spare. When judged right, the mould is allowed to drain completely into the casting slip, and a note is made of the time taken from filling to emptying for repetition purposes. The drying of the cast should be watched, and, when shrinkage from the mould is apparent, the clay in the spare can be removed and the cast loosened by tapping the mould. The mould is then untied, the sections eased apart and the cast removed. It is still plastic and easily damaged at this stage and should be put on a clean bat to harden, the mould being bound for refilling or drying out.

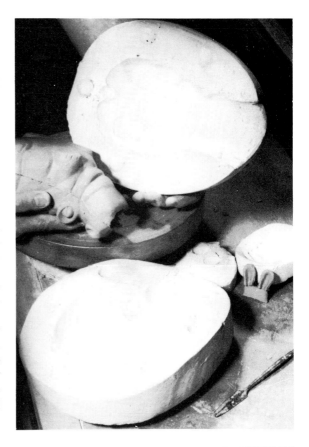

4 Assembling and fettling the cast. Casting slip should be used for the joining together of moulded sections immediately they have been removed from the mould. Apart from attaching the separately cast parts of a model, there is considerable latitude for modifying the design while the clay is still in a plastic state. Figures cast in one plane can be changed into complicated positions which would be very awkward to mould. The final fettling or cleaning up of seam marks can be done when the model is dry. The hippo was designed and moulded by Kay Keast.

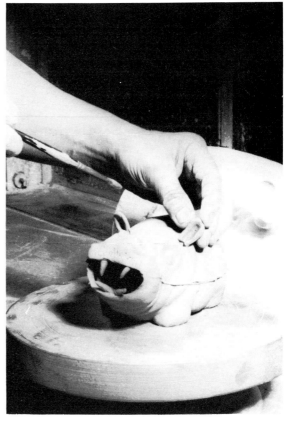

Coiling

Coiling was a natural development from the small pinched pot. To become larger it needed more clay, and for this both hands had to be free. The idea may have sprung from the technique of inverting a bowl over a pebble, or an old broken dish or basket may have suggested suitable bases on which to start; turning the work must have been almost automatic as clay was added in pieces or strips.

Coiled pots are naturally larger than pinched ones; sometimes they are huge, such as those made by the Minoans and Egyptians for the storage of grain. When size made it difficult for the potter to turn the pot on its base, he had to turn instead, round the growing pot. Although the sticking of one coil of clay on another is so simple, it is surprising in how many ways it can be done. In *Ceramics for the Archaeologist* Anna O. Shepard describes several methods used by the Indians of Central America.

In coiling it is essential that the joins should be sound. There is always a tendency to crack along joins and with so many there is a high potential cause of flaws. These often appear after the first firing, and especially when, instead of constructing a sound wall, the coils are left for their decorative effect, which tends to be unsatisfactory and weak anyway.

Coiling is a slow, sure method offering certain advantages: precise control over the thickness of the wall, the use of less plastic or roughly textured bodies, and the opportunity for bold generous decorative treatment, using free incising, inlaying, sprigging, or painting. Such decoration can be combined with raw slip glazes, brushed or sprayed onto the unfired pot, and the slip glaze itself can be cut or painted. For this reason, coiled pots are admirably suited to once firing, and the slip glazes have the advantage that they do not require the same care in handling that other glazes would need when sprayed on.

Coils can be rolled either between the hands or with the hands on a flat surface. Primitive rolling of coils had to be done without the use of a bench top. The hands on their own can extrude by rolling and funnelling quite long coils of clay thinly and evenly. This action seems to anticipate that of the present-day extruding dod-box, a device which squeezes coils out through a die and is threatening to replace the skill of coil-making in class workshops. Coils can be started between the hands and made longer and thinner on the bench.

Coiling combined with slicing is the method by which irregular ceramic sculptural forms are built. Armatures, the supports normally used in sculpture modelling, are not suitable: when the clay became firm, it would split as it shrank on them and they would have to be removed before firing. Large solid forms would also crack in the firing. But these can of course be cut in two with a wire, hollowed out, and stuck together again while still plastic. It should not be forgotten that in doing this a small hole must be left to allow for the expansion of air during the firing, otherwise the piece will burst. However, terracotta and ceramic sculpture are best built as self-supporting hollow structures, conceived from the inside as much as from the outside.

The main technical problem is to keep the whole model in a consistent, soft and workable state until it is completed, adding slab and pinched parts when they have stiffened to the same degree as the main structure. Any colour and surface treatment is an integral part of the design and should be considered from the very beginning. Coarsely grogged bodies with low shrinkage are the most suitable and safest in firing, which should begin with a slow drying-out period because moisture can still linger in thick sections after they appear to be dry.

Irregular coiled forms

Ideas for large and irregular coiled forms should be explored first through a variety of drawings and models. This enables comparison and a clear concept in the round before committing time and material to a full-sized design in which uncertainty and mistakes could prove wasteful: (*top, left to right*) four-lobed form (ED); spiked form, bottle, three-piece composite, bird form, and tall lily form (MK); large three-lobed form (EK); cylinder (RT); and squat bottle (ZF).

Preparation of coils

1 Making a coil in the hands. This is done by a slow steady application of pressure mainly from the lower edges of the hands.

2 The soft clay is funnelled down as it is rolled firmly and slowly, the size of the coil being determined by the pressure. Lengths down to the feet are possible.

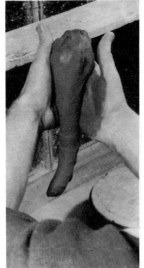

3 Rolling on a flat surface. Thick coils made by hand can be finished more thinly on the bench. The bench top should be un-

4 polished so that the clay does not stick. Splayed fingers, not the palms of the hands, should be used, starting in the middle of the coil and moving outwards.

Coiling a pot

1 Making the base. First the bat on which the pot is to be made is secured to the wheel by pressing clay round its edges. The pot can then be removed on the bat without harm for damp storage, leaving the wheel available for other work. The base is made by batting out a ball of clay with the edge of the hand to make a slice about half an inch thick. It should be trimmed if not quite circular and made level.

2 Starting the coiling. The coil is held well above the wheel in the left hand so that it hangs down to the right hand on the far edge of the base, slightly right of centre. Here the right thumb is nipping the end of the coil into the base at the edge, with all the fingers grouped on the outside to take the pressure. The clay is soft enough to stick and, as the wheel is turned by the action of coiling, the left hand feeds the coil to the right which nips it on—a thumbful at a time. Once the first revolution has been completed, the action becomes an overlapping one, each thumbful being pressed on and inside the coil below.

3 The first coil has been completed, and the pattern of thumb nipping and overlapping is clearly seen. This method has two advantages. There is a large area of bonding, above and inside each coil, and at the same time the pinching makes the wall thinner.

4 Immediately each coil is finished it should be thoroughly smoothed over on the inside. This should be done by drawing a finger or the thumb of the right hand evenly and firmly over the inside, across the coils and along them, while supporting the outside of the coiled wall with the left hand. There are two reasons for doing this. First, it strengthens the bond while the clay is still soft. Second, in continuously turning or spinning the wheel to do this, the shape can be made regular, care being taken not to stretch the wall, but to keep it inside the final profile.

5 When several coils have been added, the outside can be smoothed thoroughly by drawing the thumb vertically and diagonally across them. As the wheel turns, the final shape of the pot should be kept in mind and now that the clay has become firmer the wall can be stretched from inside, but not quite to the full profile as yet. There is still a likelihood of a sag developing which, having started, could quickly get out of hand and be difficult to correct.

6 The shape is now developing with the stretching out and expanding of the wall. The surface can be improved with scraping tools, such as a toothed template, or rib, made of metal. As before, spinning the wheel and holding the tool steadily and lightly against the clay wall will reveal irregularities in the shape as well as discrepancies in its surface. The toothed edge of the scraper should be alternated with a plain edge.

7 The shape has now grown over the shoulder to the base of the neck. The coiling has been continued still well within the design in mind and gradually stretched from inside by the smoothing of the coils. The clay is now considerably firmer, though not hard, but it can still respond to being smoothed outwards. A flat piece of wood or bat is being used to regulate the curve of the shoulder, the back of the hand acting as an anvil on the inside. This is similar to the technique of planishing in metalwork, which levels off the irregularities arising from the hammering of the metal. Without the support on the inside the wall can be tapped inwards to close the shape around the base of the neck.

8 Here a section of the pot has been cut away to show how, even at this stage, the pot can be stretched if necessary. The rounded handle of a long screwdriver will do the job and this handy tool can also be used on the outside for hollow curves.

9 Putting the lip on and shaping it to make a strong termination to the pot. After levelling the edge of the pot the lip is made with a thicker coil. The whole pot is still not too hard for altering its shape, from inside or out. While it is in this state it can be incised, inlayed, sprigged, or decorated with sgraffito either in slip or slip glaze. A coiled pot should be built regularly and evenly with quite a thin wall which needs very little if any clay removed from the outside.

An alternative method of applying coils is to lay each one on top of the one below, using slip to make sure that there is a good bond. Instead of an ascending spiral, a single complete circle is made, and this has the advantage of keeping the lip level. However, this method by its action of pressing each coil downwards on the one below tends to thicken the wall. Smoothing in is done in the same way after each coil.

Pressing and coiling combined

1 Here the roller is shown being used to lay a large slice of clay in position on the mould. The slice is lifted onto the roller by means of the canvas, which is then peeled off.

2 Building up the side of a shallow moulded dish. The strip used for this purpose was cut from the edge of the dish, lifted into position on the lip, and stuck with slip. As it comes from the same slice of clay there will be no question of its shrinking differently from the rest of the dish.

3 The same dish with the rim wall trimmed down, shaped inwards and slightly thickened to make it stronger and more interesting. Dish moulds can be used as a base on which to coil wide open pots with rounded bottoms. Coiling should begin as soon as the slice is laid in the mould, and the mould is best made and kept damp to prevent the base drying too quickly.

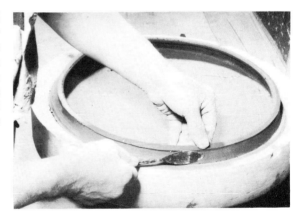

Making a large lid such as that for a bread bin. Here again the outer edge of a moulded dish has been used. The piece is lifted into position about half an inch away from the edge to make the lip which fits inside the bread bin. When sufficiently firm, the lid can be turned over onto a convex mould to retain its shape while a handle is added. Care is necessary here to see that the handle is as stiff as the lid so that it does not crack at the join in drying.

Throwing and turning

Although woman is credited with being the first potter, man appears to have taken over when the craft was mechanized. Recent trends in Africa seem to confirm this pattern: while coiling and open firing were the customary method, women were the potters, but men became interested when the wheel and kiln were introduced. Specialization, the formation of secret craft guilds, and itinerant potter families may have been contributory factors to this tendency in early history.

Once a free-turning pivoted base was devised, it could not have been long before slow dry coiling became fast wet throwing. The acceleration in pace is clearly revealed in the character of the thrown pot–a dynamic spontaneous flow compared to the static quietness of the coiled shape. The fast wheel develops a centrifugal force or 'throw', which is countered by the opposing centripetal action of the hands, creating the appearance of movement and growth in the inert clay. The skilled thrower has learnt to harness this power from the spinning wheel, using weight rather than muscular strength to counter it in the right place. This is perhaps the most direct, intimate and spontaneous way of shaping clay, and in a fascinating craft, it is probably the most bewitching process. It is the free movement of the expanding and contracting spiral which gives vitality to the thrown pot. This is not a mere surface texture, but a part of the structure of the clay wall and completely absent in an industrial pot.

A throwing body needs to be relatively smooth and soft, roughened not more than with ordinary white sand or fine grog. The action of throwing is basically the same as in pinching, but the pace is much quicker and it is faster still in industrial jollying with template and mould. More precision is required in the rounding off or centring of the lump, and the penetration, opening, raising and thinning of the wall must be steady and firm.

It is only by thorough preparation of the clay body and continual disciplined practice that skill and sensitivity in throwing are acquired. Practice is best done with several fist-sized lumps of the same weight ready to hand; each is then thrown in a strictly limited time to the same shape. By removing each effort after the specified time, say two minutes, directness of action is encouraged through the elimination of unnecessary and laboured handling. Clay soon announces its fatigue to the labouring student who keeps on playing with it.

Throwing is made possible by the use of water to lubricate the interaction of fingers and clay. No more water should be used than is necessary since too much will soften the clay, and, as skill develops, less and less will be needed. However, with large or tall pieces, finger dipping is not enough: a smooth throwing action would be made impossible because of the frequent interruptions. In these cases, water should be fed onto the lip to feed the whole surface.

When several pieces of the same size are to be made a throwing gauge can be used to check the proportions. The gauge is simply a flexible rubber tip attached to a piece of wood. It is held by a lump of clay, most conveniently on the far left of the wheel, and should be fixed after the first piece has been thrown to size. The rubber tip should just miss the lip of the pot, this usually being enough to determine its size. Each subsequent piece will be judged correct when its lip reaches the same point.

Turning is the final trimming of the foot of a thrown pot, when any superfluous clay is removed and a specially-shaped foot rim is cut. It is important that the section should not show an excessive or sudden thickening as this can cause cracking because of an abrupt variation in expansion and contraction through heat. Throwing can be sufficiently skilled to make turning unnecessary, the base being simply pressed in to make it hollow and therefore more stable: bases should always be slightly hollow, not only because the pot stands better but because a flat base has a tendency to warp outwards. However, a turned foot can add dignity and finish to a pot.

Pots are turned when they have become leather hard. As soon as thrown pots are firm enough they should be inverted to dry off evenly, otherwise the lip would dry hard first and be vulnerable to the slightest pressure when being fixed to the wheel again for turning. A dry lip would crack very easily and go undetected until it was revealed in the biscuit firing. Once the pots have been turned, they should have a light wipe over with a damp sponge or a dry nylon-fibre scouring pad, paying particular attention to the lip and foot. They should then be put on shelves, again inverted to prevent warping, for a final even drying out.

One of the requirements in making pots is the need, at various stages, to keep them damp so that they are in a soft or a leather-hard state ready for further treatment. In turning or coiling, for example, this is often necessary, especially in class workshops. Special damp-cupboards are used for this purpose, but large coiled pots are often wrapped in plastic sheeting.

The throwing wheel

A general view of the throwing wheel, showing an efficient organisation of the working area. This is an electrically driven wheel with a variable-speed foot control. It is more important for a wheel to be capable of a steady slow speed rather than an excessively fast one.

In the corner of the trough, near the right hand, which will feed water onto the clay when required, there is a bowl of water. On the left is a cutting wire with a toggle at each end so that it can hang on the edge of the trough. Next are some bats for carrying work. These vary from individual ones to long pot-boards, holding a dozen or more pieces, which require special racks with adjustable pegs near the wheel. An easily-made throwing gauge is next, ready for fixing if required in a lump of clay on the left. Behind is a pot of tools. Then, within easy reach, there is the supply of clay, wedged, weighed, and covered with a plastic sheet to keep it damp. On the right are a sponge, a needle in a holder, a throwing tool for trimming, and a pair of callipers. Various other tools are sometimes needed, but the working area should be kept as uncluttered as possible.

In Western countries, potters' wheels turn anti-clockwise, and work is done on the right-hand side in throwing and turning. Here a ball of clay is being thrown down onto the wheel-head, which is clean and dry: clay would not stick well to a wet surface. The left hand is ready to take up its position for centring.

33

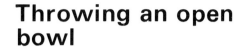

Throwing an open bowl

Centring

1 In centring, the wheel turns as fast as possible, and its power is used by opposing its anti-clockwise motion, applying pressure forward with the left hand and pulling on the right. With the weight against the left elbow, pressure passes through the forearm into the cupped hand to become effective in the base of the thumb and the heel of the hand. The right hand, also cupped, pulls the clay towards the left. Centring requires weight, not strength, in the right place, keeping body and fingers relaxed. Water is fed onto the clay with the right hand.

2 The pressure, if applied correctly, makes the clay rise in a cone; it is then shifted up into the base of each thumb to close the cone to a neat rounded point. The fingers of the left hand should be inside those of the right.

3 Pressing the cone down into the ball. The left hand remains in the same position and controls the swelling of the ball as the right hand presses the cone down. The right hand, still cupped, applies pressure on the top left of the cone, using the base of the thumb. Here the right hand is pushing against the turn of the wheel; very little pressure is needed if the action is done properly. Water should be liberally applied when learning this technique, less being necessary as skill develops.

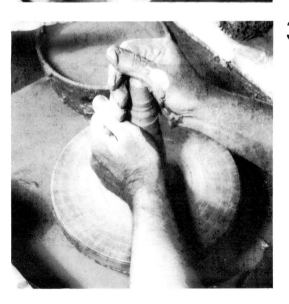

4 The downward pressure on the cone continues and the ball grows. The left hand must be kept firmly in position to stop the clay from going off centre, concentrating the weight in the heel of the hand.

5 The ball of clay is now centred. The right hand is not so cupped, having adjusted itself to the fuller shape of the ball. Cupping the hand should be instinctive to get the pressure through the base of the thumb and the lower edge of the palm.

6 When the clay is properly centred it should be nicely rounded like a dome. This can be judged by eye—the clay no longer wobbles—as well as by the feel of the hand. The dome is then flattened and slightly hollowed with the edge of the right hand, the left still in position and supporting the ball, which is now ready for opening. The right hand will continue to feed water onto the clay when needed.

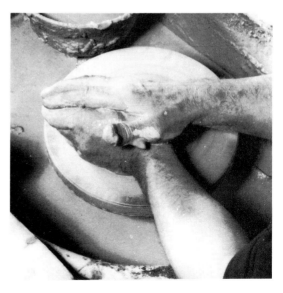

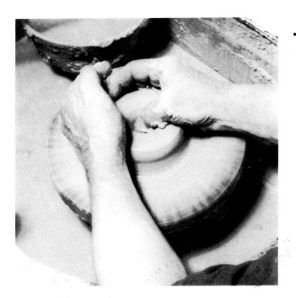

Opening the ball

7 The wheel is still turning fast, and the action is done with the right thumb. Both hands should close comfortably round the ball, riding lightly on the wheel. The right thumb feels for the middle of the ball, and with a gentle but steady pressure pushes down into the clay. The urge to follow the thumb by lifting the rest of the hand should be resisted because the hand is much steadier if kept down on the wheel. Only experience can decide how far to penetrate into the ball, but obviously the thumb must not go right through, unless plant pots are being made.

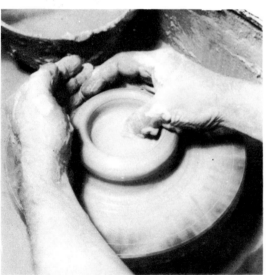

8 With the right hand still down and riding lightly on the wheel and the left hand in support, the right thumb gently and steadily applies pressure outwards against the palm without moving the hand itself. In other words, the clay wall is squeezed thinner between the thumb and the palm. With practice this should be done so that a gently curved bottom is shaped as the thumb moves from the centre. The result is a thick bowl from which a thinner one will be made to grow.

Raising the wall

9 The wheel should now turn more slowly, at about half speed. The position of both hands changes, but the right hand continues to thin the wall of clay and make it grow upwards, steadied by the left hand. With the right elbow resting on the rim of the trough, the right wrist is raised just above the right-hand edge of the bowl, and the fingers and thumb drop into position exactly as for the pinched pot method, the thumb inside and all the fingers grouped together outside. Starting right at the base of the wall, the clay is gently and equally pinched between a broad thumb-tip and the fingers.

10 As the wheel turns the pressure is raised spirally to the lip so that the whole wall is thinned evenly. The left hand is used to keep the right hand steady, not to apply pressure directly to the clay. This is done entirely by the right hand, which develops a sense of the thickness and feel of the clay wall between thumb and fingers.

11 The throwing or pinching up of the clay wall continues, starting from the bottom each time so that the clay is actually raised. When approaching the lip, the pressure should relax just enough to make a slight fullness here, and the thumb and finger should stop short of the lip so that it remains nicely rounded, not thin and sharp, which can make it split.

This view from the other side shows the position of the right hand. For clarity the left hand has been moved, but it would normally be supporting the right.

The bowl, showing its section and again the position of the right hand, thumb, and fingers. Note the curve inside the bottom of the bowl, the thickness of the base, and the rounded lip.

Finishing off

1 The hand has a natural template for finishing the lip of the bowl. By using the space between the index and second fingers, the lip can be perfectly rounded off and made clean of slurry and the sharp ridges which form when the fingertips are used.

2 The sponging out of the water before the bowl is removed from the wheel. A natural sponge is best, otherwise a fine-textured synthetic one should be used. Water must be removed; if left, the bottom would become soft and the pot could not dry evenly.

3 Surplus clay should be trimmed from the base on the outside, cutting well under the pot at the same time to make lifting off easier.

Taking off

1 First, the pot must be cut off the wheel with the wire. This should be held taut, the wire being wound round the index fingers and pressed on the wheel by the thumbs, as close to the wheel as possible so that there is no danger of its rising into the pot.

2 Placing the fingers in position ready to lift the pot off. The index and second fingers of each hand are spread under and round the base on each side, spanning it as far as possible.

3 The pot should be lifted off by peeling from one side, not by raising the entire pot at once. Many pots are spoiled in the way they are lifted off. If the undercutting with the trimming tool has given a clear space at the base for the fingers to get right under the pot, there should be no difficulty. Pots should be put on dry bats so that they do not stick and can shrink in drying.

Throwing a cylinder

1 The wheel should be turning fast. Here a larger lump of clay has been used, the centring has been completed, the lump penetrated with the thumb, and the pulling out or opening has begun. Centring and penetration proceed as for the throwing of a bowl, but the opening is different. Instead of curving the bottom as for a bowl, the clay has been pulled out horizontally and much wider so that a wide shallow cone has taken shape. This is because cylinders are easier to raise if the mouth is kept smaller than the base. They are wide or tall according to the proportions of the required pot.

2 The wide shallow cone has been closed into a smaller and slightly taller one. The position of the hands is not unlike that in centring when the solid lump is pushed up into a cone. The same parts of the hands are used, cupped to concentrate the pressure on the base of the thumb and the edge of the palm, but the clay is also supported here by the fingers. The wheel is still turning fast.

3 Raising the wall of clay. The wheel is reduced to about half speed. The lifting of the clay wall is effected in basically the same way as for a bowl, by pressure on both sides, but this time inwards not outwards. Here, in the most usual method, the left fingertips are on the inside, all grouped together, and the knuckle of the right index finger is on the outside. Starting at the bottom, the clay is supported on the inside by the fingertips and pressed on the outside with the knuckle. See also Figure 1a; 1b–3 illustrate an alternative method, with the right thumb replacing the knuckle on the outside and the index finger just behind to steady the hand. The position illustrated in 1b is also used to make a very narrow cylinder.

4 As the hands are raised, the wall grows upwards, inwards, and thinner. Here this is being done for the second time and the conical cylinder is straightening. The knuckle and fingertips are not always exactly opposite each other but this variation will be acquired with experience. For the time being let them be opposite. Contact is maintained by keeping the left thumb touching the right hand as long as possible. The pressure is on the near, not the far, side; this makes for a steadier position. Water is fed onto the rim so that it runs down to feed the fingers and knuckle. See Figures 2 and 3, which show how in the bellying out and closing of a cylinder outside pressure closes the throat over inside support at the shoulder.

5 Closing in a lip or collaring (see Figure 4). Here the movement started at the shoulder of the cylinder. The left hand is now outside, adding a light pressure on the right, but pressure is still applied on the inside, with the right index finger, while the knuckle of the right second finger and the two thumbs, out of sight, help to close the collar. The mopping out of the water and the trimming of the clay away from the base proceed as for the bowl before the cutting off is done and the pot lifted off.

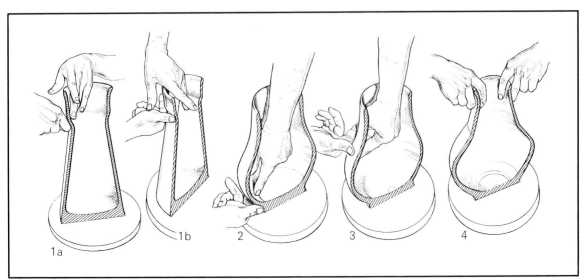

1a   1b   2   3   4

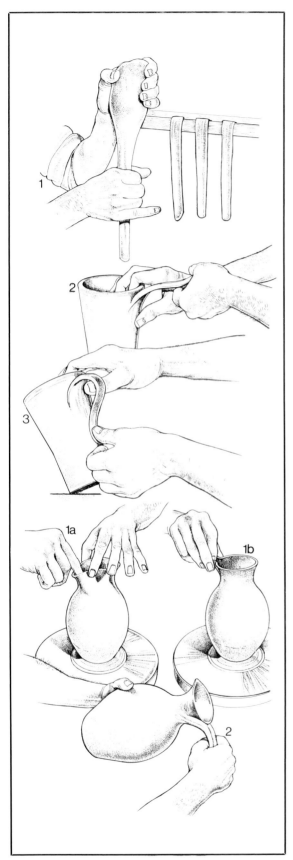

Handles

1 Fist-sized lumps of well-wedged clay are tapered and wet-pulled downwards between thumb and index finger. For a sure grip, the section should be oval, the underside tending to be flat from the straight thumb: round sections look heavy, flat thin ones weak. Tapering gives a feeling of growth. Here the strips are being nipped off onto a shelf to stiffen slightly before being bent to shape on the pot, but they can be bent ready before stiffening.

2 & 3 Attaching the handle. It is imperative that handle and pot are equally soft. When they are still tacky a good bond is assured; when leather hard, slip on a keyed (scratched) surface is necessary; joining is very uncertain when pots are hard. Here a soft handle is shaped as it is attached to a tacky mug, the thicker end first, at the top.

Jugs

Spouts are best made on fresh-thrown pots.

1a & b Alternative methods of making a spout: a wet index finger pouting out the lip between the other index finger and thumb, and a similar action using the fingers of one hand.

2 A handle can be pulled off the pot from a firmly attached lump (not limited to jugs).

Teapots

1 Raising the cone to make the spout after opening at the top of a lump.

2 Final shaping.

3 Nipping off with the thumb. This can also be done with a tool or wire.

4 Shaping the inside flange with a square tool.

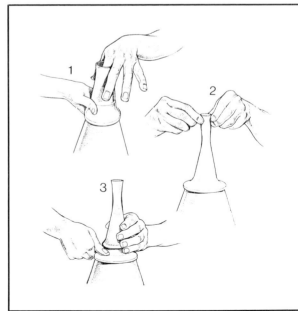

The thick lip has been split and the flange is being pressed down, while the left hand supports the lip. The mouth should be slightly smaller than required; it is adjusted last of all.

5 Once the base of the spout has been cut to fit the belly of the pot, its position is marked and the gridholes are drilled. Their total area should be greater than that of the mouth of the spout to ensure a good pour.

6 Joining pot and spout. The clay is leather hard, and a good join is made by scoring, slipping, and firmly pressing the spout on.

7 The end of the spout is trimmed with a sharp knife. It must not be lower than the mouth, otherwise the pot will overflow when filled. The handle is attached last to give balance to the pot.

Lids

Lids are best thrown on top of a large lump.

1 & 2 A lid being thrown for a turned or attached knob. Once a shallow bowl with a thick lip has been thrown slightly smaller than necessary, the lip is split with the little finger, which presses the flange down level with the inside of the bowl; the vertical lip should lean inwards, and the diameter of the opening must be adjusted to the required size. The lid is nipped or cut off leaving either enough clay from which to turn a knob, or just enough for trimming over for an attached knob.

3 & 4 A lid with a thrown knob, this being shaped first. The dished part is nipped off and, when leather hard, trimmed. This type best suits storage jars.

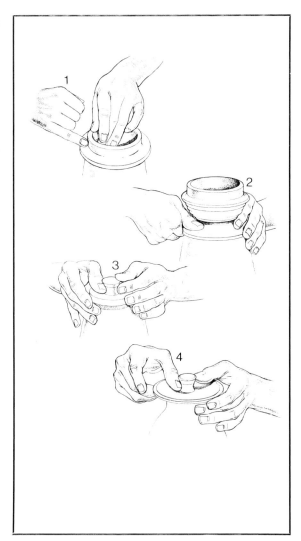

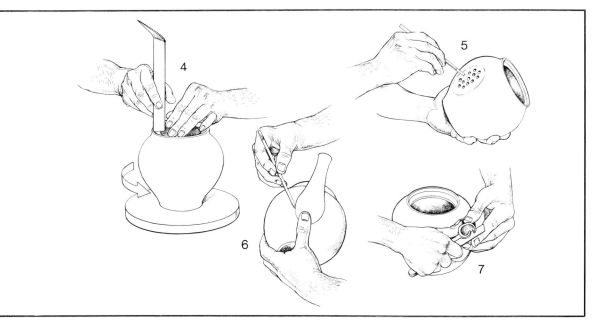

Throwing a shallow dish

1 After centring, the ball is pressed out into a large saucer shape with the edge of the right hand. This is done on the left-hand side against the turning of the wheel and steadied by the left hand. The wheel is fairly fast, as for centring.

2 With a reduced speed, the lip of the thick saucer shape is raised upwards on the outside at a steep angle from the wheel-head. An overhang must be avoided as it will tend to sag, creating a shoulder on the inside. If the base is sufficiently thick, the dish can be lifted off by trimming well under the edge with a long pointed tool, cutting with the wire and peeling from one side. The alternative is to throw on a bat and remove this with the dish. However, a wire should be passed under the dish first so that it can shrink as it stiffens and be lifted off easily. Bats are attached in various ways, soft clay sometimes being sufficient.

Turning

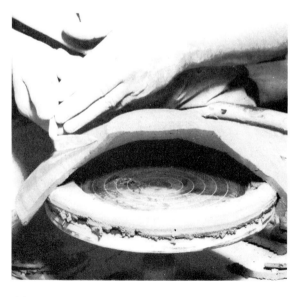

This requires knowledge of the section of the pot, the shape inside and the thickness of the wall, and comes only with practice, with the turning and bisecting of many pieces. This illustration shows in section the turning of a dish which is larger than the wheel-head. The problem of fixing is solved by resting the inside of the dish on a collar of clay attached and trued on the rim of the wheel-head.

1 Centring and fixing a smaller bowl on the wheel. The bowl is leather hard, and it is fixed to the wheel at its lip and perfectly centred so that the pot can be turned. The centring can be quite simply done as shown, by pressing a coil of clay onto the wheel, cutting it to fit close to the rim of the pot, and then gently and firmly closing the clay against the rim. With practice a pot can be centred quickly by tapping it into the centre as the wheel spins.

2 The turning can be done with a variety of tools. Soft clay can be cut with wood or wire, but leather-hard clay needs a metal tool. Anything harder than leather hard is difficult to cut. Turning is best begun in the centre of the foot to establish the correct thickness and then work from that point outwards. This ensures an initial hollow which should be retained when the rest of the foot is trimmed.

3 Here the base outside the foot ring is being turned, bearing in mind the thickness at the middle and the profile on the inside of the pot.

4 The foot ring being given a final burnish with the other end of the tool. Since this part of the pot will not be glazed, the smoother it is the better, especially with coarsely grogged bodies, which can have unpleasant effects in use if the foot is left rough.

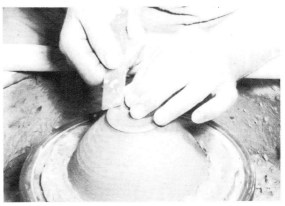

Decoration

Of all human-made objects, nothing resembles its maker or reflects her or his physical attributes more than a clay pot: a vessel with a belly, a foot and arm, a shoulder closing to throat, mouth, and lip. It can be female or male, left bare or clothed with ornament which may be simple and practical or elaborate and useless, solemnly traditional or whimsically fashionable, tastefully restrained or indulgently vulgar.

Over the centuries the accumulation of methods, styles, and materials has made decorative techniques bewilderingly complex. But basically there are three ways in which decoration can be applied to a pot: (a) by the use of clay, (b) by the use of ceramic colours, and (c) by the use of glaze.

Clay

Of these three ways, the use of clay offers most in variety and is generally most reliable. All clay treatment must of course take place before firing.

The clay surface, in all stages from soft to hard, provides considerable graphic diversity for the simple line, drawn or incised with finger, nail, or tool point – from the fluid quality of a brush to the precision of a graver. Detail can be blurred or accented with wet or dry brushing of a contrasting slip, and changed again later with the texture of glaze. Not only can the soft surface be *incised* and *impressed* with finger and tool, but with all manner of things, ready-made or specially cut, composing rich and composite images.

While soft, the pot can be *sprigged* with plain or coloured pellets or strips freely shaped and stuck directly onto the tacky surface; these can then be smudged, spread, and incised. When pressed from a plaster mould, sprigs need slip to attach them to the leather-hard clay.

Sgraffito is drawing and cutting through a layer of slip coloured differently from the body. The thinner the layer, the more spontaneous is the sgraffito, and dry-brushed slip is thinner than one poured onto leather-hard clay. Further brushing can accentuate the incised design afterwards.

Trailing is drawing with slip squeezed through a fine nozzle fitted to a rubber bulb. *Feathering* is drawing a point or a feather through a pattern of slip which has been trailed on a layer of contrasting slip while it is still fluid. With several coloured slips, a fine intricate pattern or marbling is produced, with sharp definition.

Contrasting *clay inlay* can be a wet filling using slip or a stiff filling using clay in a leather-hard surface. In wet filling the slip is brushed freely onto the impressed or incised clay surface, and while still wet the surplus is scraped with a rubber kidney. Stiff inlay first requires the precise engraving of channels with a vee-section lino cutter. The channels should be damped before they are filled, to make a good bond with the stiff clay spills of the contrasting inlay body. The clay used for inlaying should be as stiff as possible to avoid any cracking due to shrinking in the channels. Scraping with a steel blade to clean up a design should not proceed until the inlayed body is firm and hard, making a precise pattern without smudging.

Stencils and *wax resist* are similar in that they both protect selected areas from the application of slip or colour. Thin paper stencils can be hard edged with scissor cutting or soft edged with tearing. Damp tissue will lie close to a leather-hard surface, and coloured slip can be poured on and allowed to dry off before the stencil is removed. Damped paper will stick sufficiently to a dry surface for the spraying or brushing on of slip, which dries more quickly. Wax emulsion can be freely painted onto a dry surface and is soon firm enough for brushing over with coloured slip, which is repelled by the wax. On a leather-hard surface the wax takes rather longer to set, but slip can then be poured over it.

Ceramic colours

Apart from oxides themselves (see page 7), a wide range of prepared colours and stains are available from potters' suppliers. There are different preparations for use as under-glaze or on-glaze decoration, for earthenware and stoneware, and for body and glaze colouring. No harm can come from experimental interchange, but some earthenware colours are not likely to survive a high temperature.

Under-glaze work is applied directly onto the biscuit or body. Oxides and colours applied to the raw body will still rub off after biscuit firing and should therefore be mixed with slip instead of water to fix them. Another way of preventing colours being smudged on biscuit (or being washed away when glazing) is to dissolve a little gum in the water in which they are mixed. The water should be just tacky between the thumb and finger: too much gum will resist the glaze.

Under-glaze designs show most clearly under transparent glazes, coloured ones modifying them, and opaque and matte glazes subduing them more or less according to the glaze thickness. During firing, colours do not remain stationary but can permeate body and glaze, rising to the surface of a thin glaze.

On-glaze colours are usually applied to the unfired glaze, an opaque white one called maiolica generally being used in earthenware for brightness. Opaque white glazes are often used on stoneware for the same reason, but on-glaze colours can be used on darker glazes, producing an intense and metallic quality in earthenware and especially with late reduction on stoneware glazes (see page 49).

Painting on the unfired glaze must be sure and skilled, correction being impossible without ruining the glaze layer. This difficulty is often overcome in maiolica painting by firing the glaze first; designs can then be corrected easily but this method makes another glost firing necessary.

One of the first facts learned in the use of colouring oxides is their widely differing degrees of intensity. It requires, for example, as much as five parts of iron oxide to equal the colour intensity of one part of cobalt. But even apart from this no two oxides are quite the same in behaviour. Prepared colours may be more alike in behaviour, but the knowledge and judgement necessary in glazing can only come through trial and error.

The range and brightness of prepared colours and oxides tend to become more limited as the firing temperature rises. In earthenware, there is a fairly wide range available, but it is not as brilliant as the range of enamel colours firing at just under 800°C. Enamel colours and metallic lustres are really soft frits or glazes. They are applied in a variety of ways onto the fired glaze, usually on white earthenware and china, and require a third low firing. On stoneware and raku they give a jewel-like quality which is in contrast to the texture of a coarse body. At stoneware temperatures, colours and oxides lose in brilliance but gain in depth and subtlety.

The application of colour should not be limited to painting with a simple brush. The way should be open to any tool, and to any method which succeeds in creating new kinds of pattern, such as trailing, resist, spraying, or offset printing from any absorbent material like cloth, sponge, string, the soft torn edge of cardboard, or even the fingers.

Selected glazes and oxides (see back cover)
A1 Clear colourless glaze over lead antimoniate, and cobalt, manganese, copper and red iron oxides; lower edge unglazed.
2 Tin glaze with the same oxides on glaze (copper and cobalt reversed).
3 Copper and manganese under clear glaze.
4 Copper and manganese on tin glaze.
5 Clear glaze over green (copper) slip and red slip; lower half clouded, being thick.
6 Alkaline turquoise glaze with copper, and honey Wrotham slip glaze over red slip.
7 Wrotham slip glaze over black, white, and blue slip.
8 Iron and copper stained glazes over black inlay, glazes overlapping on the left.

B1–5 Glazes over blue, red, black, and green slips; top unglazed, middle thin, bottom thick.
1 Clear colourless. **2** Tin. **3** Titanium. **4** Dolomite. **5** Lithium and barium.
6 Clear glaze over red and green slips; top edge unglazed.
7 Dolomite glaze over black and blue slips; bottom unglazed.
8 Lithium and barium glaze with copper and under-glaze copper.
9 Clear glaze over iron; slight speckle from fireclay in body.

C1 Clear glaze over copper with red reduction.
2 Clear glaze over iron, oxide breaking through.
3 Titanium glaze over black and blue slips.
4 Dolomite glaze over crocus martis.
5 Thin lithium glaze over copper.
6 Clear glaze over red and green slips (same as B6), cloudy where thick.
7 Dolomite glaze over black and blue slips (same as B7).
8 Same as B8; thick glaze and oxide blisters.
9 Same as B9; stronger speckle.
10 Matte celadon; pronounced speckle.

Use of glazes

Glazes vary in two ways, in texture and in colour. There may be innumerable transitional textures, but for general purposes there are three: shiny, matte or dry. Shiny glazes are transparent, allowing pattern to show through, but they tend to become cloudy when thick. Matte and dry glazes on the other hand are opaque, and pattern will show through in varying degrees according to the thickness both of the glaze and of the colour, remembering colour often permeates and rises in firing.

Glazes are modified by the addition of stains and oxides, either as colours or as opacifiers, which are white. Thus a transparent glaze can be coloured green and remain transparent, or be made opaque with tin oxide.

Glazes subdue under-glaze decoration in various ways and create contrast in colour and texture when parts of the design are missed by half dipping, wax resist or stencil. Indeed contrasts with considerable decorative value of their own are produced by using various glazes in this way on plain bodies. Part dipping and overlapping of one glaze creates a pattern of varying textures, different degrees of opacity and intensity of colour. And when two glazes, differing in colour or texture or both, are used in this way, there is a rich permutation. Mottled patterning occurs with a light glaze overlapping a dark one, and vice versa.

Rich pattern is produced by sgraffito in light opaque glaze over a coloured slip or oxide, also with wax resist. Scratching through a thin glaze when still damp produces fine precise lines; coarse and ragged lines result when the glaze is thick and dry. Wax resist can also be applied on-glaze and colour brushed over, producing a darker contrast on a light opaque glaze.

Crackle can be a feature of high-temperature ware, which is vitrified, and is caused by the crazing of a glaze which does not fit the body. With non-porous pots this does not constitute a fault as it would in earthenware, which would leak as a result. Crackle can be accentuated by rubbing or washing in colour and refining if wished, but more unstained crackle is likely to emerge.

Unglazed clay treatments
1 Finger drawn and tool impressed.
2 Slip trailing and feathering.
3 Tool incised and black slip dry-brushed.
4 Sprigging with white body on dark ground.
5 Sgraffito through black slip.
6 Inlay of black body in white.

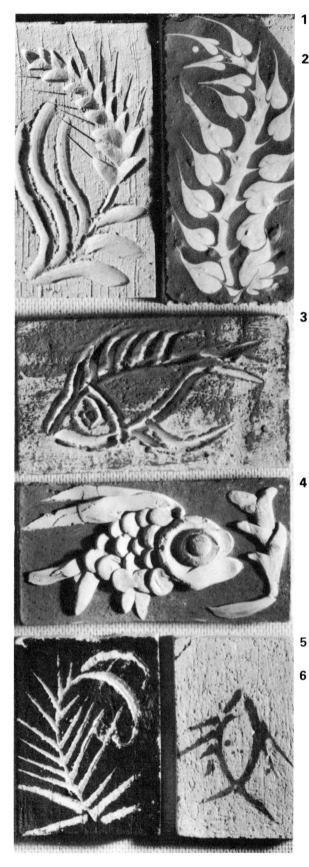

Firing and glazing

Introduction

No pottery is possible without the means of heating clay to at least about 700–800° C by which time it has become a cherry-red colour. Neolithic potters were able to make pottery because the spread of vegetation during that period provided fuel. But it was many thousands of years before an efficient means of raising temperatures to a sustained white heat was achieved, first by potters in China. Today we take it for granted that we can fire a pot merely by pressing a switch, all that is needed to start a modern electric kiln. This method of firing has only been developed in the last fifty years and has already transformed the conditions under which the craft can be practised. The kiln's compact size, its portability, and efficient insulation make it useable in the home, literally alongside the cooker, where, after all, pottery started over 20,000 years ago.

At that time pots were fired quite simply in an open fire, probably in a shallow pit. Primitive potters still use this method these days in various parts of the world where electrical power or gas and other fuels are not available in ready and continuous supply. The pots which were fired in this haphazard way were not very hard, and they were unglazed and affected by variations in the fire – black with smoke and red where the fire was bright. Uneven firing caused a large proportion of spoiled pots. Gradually the open-pit fire became a kiln: first with the addition of a low wall to concentrate and contain the area, later a higher wall which sloped up to a domed roof, then a floor supported on props over the fire, and finally a chimney. This single-chambered up-draught kiln continued to be used and modified in the West, but not with the success of the many-chambered, down-draught climbing kiln of the Far East. Developed from a cave dug in the side of an earth bank,

this gave better draught control, more rapid and complete combustion, and eventually very high temperatures.

A draught is the natural upward movement of hot air, expanding and rising in a column through surrounding cold air. In the early Western type of kiln, heat rises as an up-draught to an opening in the top. However, it can be drawn to an opening near the bottom, thus making a down draught, provided this opening leads directly to a chimney which rises well above the top of the kiln chamber. In the Eastern climbing kiln, several down-draught chambers are connected, the second slightly above the first and so on, like a continuous chimney.

Kilns using solid fuels, or oil or gas, are heated by combustion. This is the combining of carbon and oxygen after they have been ignited. As long as both last, combustion will continue. Sufficient oxygen ensures complete combustion, all carbon being consumed or burned, and a clean or oxidising atmosphere is produced. Too much carbon or insufficient oxygen results in incomplete combustion and a smoky or reducing atmosphere. Unconsumed carbon combines with any oxide it contacts at a high temperature and thus affects those in the pottery, particularly colours.

Electric kilns are heated by radiation from electrical energy conducted through special elements. As no carbon fuel is involved, electric kilns are oxidising, and reduction can be affected only by introducing carbonaceous matter into the kiln chamber at a high temperature. Generally this is not practised, except with kilns fitted with non-metallic elements, since reduction affects the metal elements and their working life is shortened by alternately oxidising and reducing.

In class workshops and studios, electric and gas kilns are in most common use because of their convenience for installation and firing.

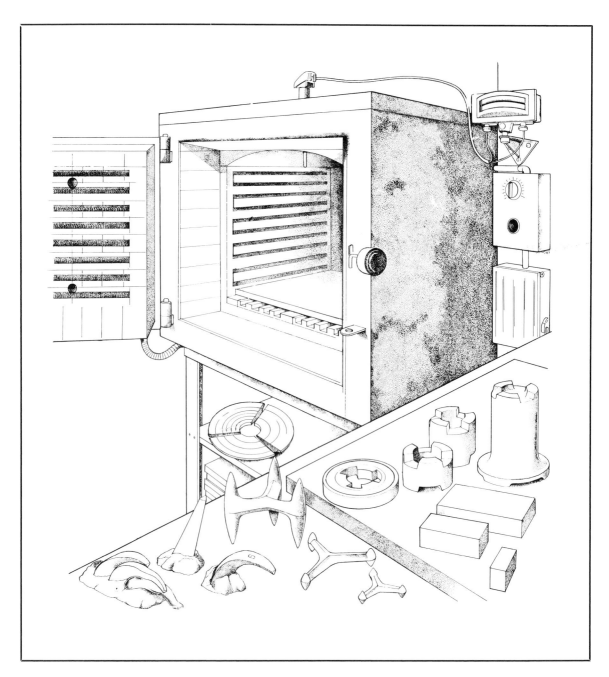

Electric kilns

The example illustrated is a front-loading model with elements in all sides and in the floor. Power is supplied through the main switch via the speed-control unit. Above the control is the pyrometer, which is connected to the pyrocouple, fitted into the top of the kiln, and which indicates kiln temperature. However, time as well as temperature is involved in firing, and pyrometric cones are a more reliable way of indicating the effect of heat on ceramic materials. They are placed in the kiln where they can be seen during the firing. In the left foreground are (a) an unfired cone in clay (centre), (b) a used cone, bent enough to indicate its specified temperature (right), and (c) a group of three, used to indicate stages in a reduction firing–(left to right) the final temperature; 30°C below it, as a warning; and the point at which reduction was begun–the two latter having of course melted further. Also shown are three porcelain stilts or spurs for supporting pots with glazed feet, a kiln shelf similar to the kiln floor, and circular and cube-shaped props. Under the kiln is an adjustable dish crank in three pieces.

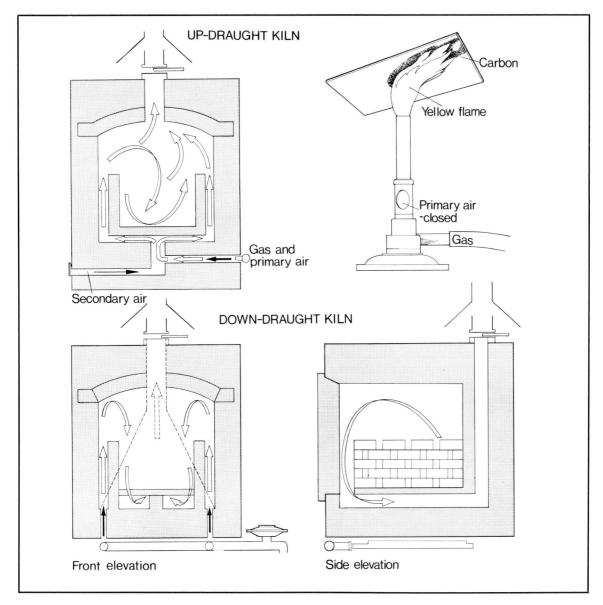

UP-DRAUGHT KILN

Carbon

Yellow flame

Primary air -closed

Gas

Gas and primary air

Secondary air

DOWN-DRAUGHT KILN

Front elevation

Side elevation

Gas kilns

Gas kilns are either of the up-draught or down-draught type. In the first, the burners are placed so that the flames enter the combustion area under the kiln-chamber floor by individual flues. Here they divide to each side and rise into the chamber, along the arched roof and out through the chimney. In a down-draught kiln, the flames rise on each side of the chamber and are then drawn forward and down under the floor and up the chimney at the rear, thus completely encircling the chamber. In either case, the chimney is fitted with a damper, which is closed on completion of the firing.

Openings near the bottom admit secondary air, to assist complete combustion. A bunsen burner clearly shows how primary and secondary air function in combustion. Air can enter at the base of the burner and mix with the gas before it burns: this is the primary air. The resulting flame is blue, indicating complete combustion. Partially closing this opening and reducing primary air causes incomplete combustion: the flame is partly yellow due to the presence of unburnt carbon (as revealed by the deposit on a cold surface held against the flame). The flame will continue when primary air is completely shut off, because of the surrounding secondary air, but will be entirely yellow.

The elevations show a semi-muffle arrangement. Low walls on each side prevent the flues from being covered with pots but permit contact between flame and work during reduction.

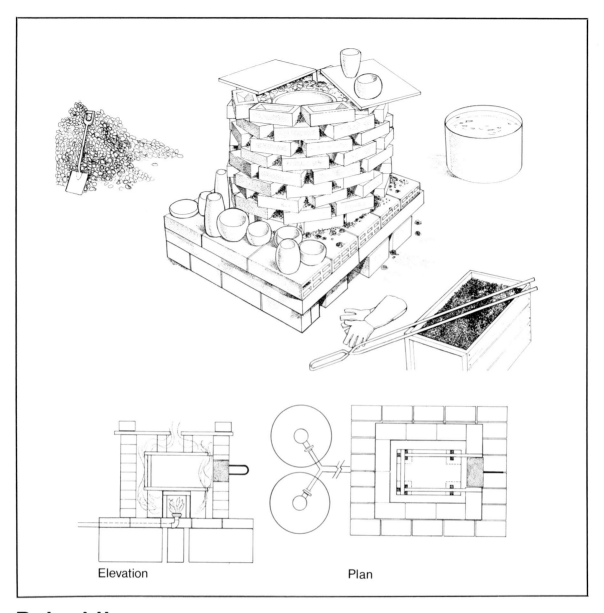

Elevation

Plan

Raku kilns

At the top is a raku setting with a kiln typical of the top-loading, coke-fired, brazier variety. The bricks are spaced and skintled to leave air vents, and the muffle rests on four bricks placed on end. Raising the kiln on a platform of spaced bricks and cement blocks results in a stronger draught, better firing, and easier stoking and side loading. Near the kiln are boxes of reduction materials, such as peat, grass, and sawdust, and a tub of water, long tongs and asbestos gauntlets. Glazes and colours should also be conveniently at hand.

Below are the elevation and plan of a kiln fired by bottle gas alone or plus solid fuel (coke or wood). The inside wall of the kiln is best made of firebricks and the outer one of house bricks, all

bedded with a fireclay-and-sand mixture. The door is a lightweight insulating brick with a metal-rod handle cemented into it.

The muffle is constructed from old kiln shelves locked together with broken pieces stuck with sillimanite cement at the corners: a muffle made in one piece is always liable to crack. The top can be used for firing tiles, and the bottom should be protected from the impact of the gas flame by placing a tile immediately underneath it. The muffle is held rigidly in position by extending the side pieces into the door cavity on the front wall of the kiln, and also by bricks on the top which support old shelves used partly to cover the kiln and as a pre-heating base for work. If gas is to be used alone, the space between muffle and walls can be reduced.

Biscuit packing and firing

Although the word 'biscuit' generally means twice baked, in pottery it is used to describe the initial firing of clay when it becomes pot. Here clay takes on a permanent state, and before this happens is perhaps the time to consider whether it is worth proceeding with the work or whether to use the clay to try to make something of a higher standard. A transformation certainly takes place in the kiln, but often not the kind that is expected. One thing is certain: the result is a very permanent one, and it is much easier to alter the work while it is still clay. The whole piece should be carefully checked for minor flaws, which spoil what is otherwise sound. The foot and lip can be made clean and regular. Uneven textures from careless or untidy handling can be removed, inside as well as out, and slight cracks at joins can still be repaired. But any piece which raises doubts is best discarded and the clay used again.

Before the biscuit packing is begun, all work must be absolutely dry so that there is no possibility of initial bursting if a piece is packed near the source of heat or is heated unevenly. In its dry clay state, a pot is fragile and easily broken by wrong or careless handling, and cannot then be repaired.

Pieces can touch each other in biscuit packing and therefore stacking together is possible. Care is necessary here to prevent undue strain on pieces which support others. Common-sense can be a good guide, but experience counts most. Some points, however, could be noted. In stacking, heavier and stronger pieces should naturally be used to support lighter and more fragile ones. But in open shapes like bowls the weight must be transferred through the feet, not the rims; any outward pressure here would cause a split. Closed and cylindrical pieces can be stacked up, provided again the heavier ones support the lighter ones. Bowls which will not quite nest on their feet inside other bowls can be supported on small props, kiln bits, or sand. Bowls can also be inverted on pots. Inverting often solves the problem of filling an awkward space, as long as the pot's lip is strong enough to take the weight. Strong cylindrical pieces can often be put on their sides but no piece should be placed at a tilt on its lip. Large open-mouthed pots can be safely filled with smaller pieces. With a mixed batch of pots of all sizes, a kiln could be packed almost without the use of shelves, large pieces occupying the lower part of the kiln and supporting smaller ones above. Flat shapes, however, do need packing separately on shelves, to avoid warping.

The kiln packed for a biscuit firing, showing a variety of pieces including tiles, saucers, cups, bowls, teapots, and a large piece inverted.

Dishes which have been decorated with slips of different colours should be separated in the stack by placing-sand to prevent the offsetting of the design onto the next dish.

After organizing the batch of work, deciding on the appropriate height of shelf props and allowing for the tallest pieces, packing should begin, by first positioning the shelf props. Shelves are best supported on three props, evenly distributed to take the weight, two in adjacent corners and the third in the middle of the opposite side. With adjacent shelves, one prop can be shared, the props being placed one in each corner and the fifth in the centre of the kiln.

Pieces are then placed in position on the floor of the kiln, tight close to each other. When packing for any kind of firing, the object is not only to fill the kiln as much as possible and not waste space, but to pack evenly, without leaving empty pockets. This is not only wasteful but it can cause unevenness in temperature. The placing of work of the same size and shape is no problem, but odd shapes and sizes need ingenuity and imagination. In an electric kiln, there should be a clearance of at least one to two inches, according to the size and shape of the work, between it and the elements; the smaller a piece is the nearer it can be. Anything closer than an inch is liable to an extra-hard firing in that part next to the element, or possibly bursting or cracking in a large piece. The same could happen in a gas kiln where there is direct contact with the flame so pieces should not be placed over the edge of a semi-muffle. When the floor has been filled, with the props showing a clearance above the work, the shelf is placed in position and pieces are packed on it. If another shelf is needed, above the first, the props should be placed immediately over the lower ones. Shelves should also have a clearance, of at least half an inch, from the elements. This is important because any element which is boxed in cannot radiate heat properly; consequently the heat builds up in a confined space and can cause overheating, and eventually burning out.

In the packing of a kiln, allowance should be made for the means of recording the temperature. Cones must be placed so that they can be observed through the spy hole. If a pyrometer is to be used, the pyrocouple will already be in position, protruding through the roof or the back wall. This is a vulnerable instrument, easily broken if knocked during packing, and it is a wise precaution to withdraw it while packing proceeds and replace it afterwards.

The kiln door should be closed and secured before firing is begun. The speed of heating must be regulated to ensure a proper rise in temperature. Controls vary on different makes of kiln, but they should enable a slow rise until a temperature of 600°C is reached, allowing for a speed of not more than 100° per hour for work of an average size. Small work can be fired more quickly, large pieces more slowly. The change from clay to pot takes place between 500°C and 600°C. At this stage dehydration occurs and the water of plasticity is released as steam. The spy holes and air vents should all remain open to permit the steam to escape. When a pyrometer is not used this provides the only indication that dehydration has taken place. Once the steaming has stopped and the pots inside the kiln are a cherry red, it is possible to increase the speed gradually to full, until the pyrometer or the cones indicate the maturing temperature required for biscuit. This is varied: 750°C for raku, 900–1020°C for stoneware and porcelain, and 1020°C upwards for earthenwares. Earthenware is biscuited harder because of a tendency for glazes to craze on soft biscuit. This is not so liable to occur in the higher firing temperatures of stoneware and porcelain.

When the firing is completed, the power or gas is switched off, the control turned to the off position, the chimney and all vents closed, and cooling allowed to proceed naturally until the work can be handled with bare hands. Biscuit is not vulnerable to cold draughts and can be allowed to cool fairly quickly, but risks should not be taken unnecessarily, particularly with large pieces such as open bowls or shallow dishes. Care is also needed to avoid any possibility of biscuit becoming soiled in handling as this can cause faults to develop in the glazing and glost firing. It should be properly stored, away from dust and unnecessary handling until required for glazing.

Glazing

After the initial firing, which changes clay into biscuit, the next stage is to glaze the pot and put it once more in the kiln for the glost firing. But first, what is a glaze?

It is not certain how the making of a glassy material originally came about; but as with the behaviour of clay, certain natural earths and minerals were observed to react in particular ways when subjected to fire. The sand of the Dead Sea was found to melt, and the early Egyptians made decorative ornaments of clay and stone coated with the resulting fused paste, which looked like natural turquoise when coloured with a copper mineral. The Indian potters of Central America found an orange earth which they painted on their pots, but discarded it when, instead of giving the same colour after firing, it turned dull brown and shiny. In more recent times, in the Middle East, the use of straw for oven fuel was found to produce a glassy crystalline ash. Through observation and patient experiment over hundreds of years, glazes of great beauty and variety were evolved, and the accumulated knowledge was handed on from one generation of craftsmen to the next, often in great secrecy.

Today these secrets are commonplaces. We know that sand melts at 1600°C and that certain earths have specific melting points, forming glassy products above those temperatures. We know that deposits of salts of soda and potash in the Dead Sea sand made it melt easily, and that the orange earth of the Indian potters was crude lead ore, which in a purer form today is one of the most effective ingredients in a glaze.

The attempt to produce some kind of order and scientific basis out of all the accumulated knowledge and recipes was made by a German chemist, Hermann Seger, whose name was given to the cones still used for measuring temperatures in the kiln. He tried to reduce each recipe to an exact chemical formula but found it impossible. His idea, however, proved sufficiently accurate for practical purposes and is used today for a more exact approach to the subject.

Nevertheless there are still some things in ceramics that are not fully understood and an air of mystery and secrecy still persists in the practice of the craft, particularly in the use of glazes. Knowledge and skill can only come from study and practice, even with the so-called 'reliable' glazes prepared by manufacturers.

It is now known that a glaze is made up of three compounds – silica, flux, and alumina. Sand is a form of silica, others being flint and quartz. Soda, potash and lead compounds are fluxing agents, and heated with silica produce glass. However, this glass is not suitable for glazing pots: it melts too much at pottery temperatures and runs off. The third compound, alumina, is used to remedy this, making the melt viscous and less fluid. Alumina is a pure form of clay, found as china clay, but all clays are mainly alumina and silica and provide two of the compounds in a glaze. Therefore glazes can be, and are, made from various clays with the addition of a flux. Other minerals are found to contain alumina, silica, and a flux. But however great the number and variety of ingredients involved, all glaze recipes can be reduced to these three basic components – flux, alumina, and silica. Chinese potters, in their emotive way, like to refer to them as blood, flesh, and bone.

As a general practice, glazes are applied to pots after they are biscuit fired. Handling a raw pot for glazing requires care and skill because clay is easily broken and the wet glaze can soften and crack thin sections. The glaze also adheres better to biscuit; a thick coat on raw clay flakes off readily and is more easily damaged. In firing, more reaction takes place between the glaze and raw clay so that firing on biscuit is more consistent.

However, glazes can be prepared specially for application to raw pots – by making a slip glaze, that is a clay slip which, with a flux, melts like a glaze. This can often be achieved by replacing either all or part of the alumina or china-clay content in a glaze recipe with a plastic clay. The glaze slip can then be applied by brushing or spraying on the dry pot and by pouring or dipping when leather-hard. There are still limitations, and perhaps the boldness of the method is best suited to large coiled pots; they can take a more robust treatment and a single firing represents a real saving in time and kiln space.

There are many variables in glazes and glost firing. Not only do materials of the same name vary and behave differently, but the wide range of clay bodies must affect identical glazes in individual ways and produce dissimilar effects. Even when bodies and glazes and colours are identical, different kilns (or even identical kilns) and conditions in firing have their influence; and even in the same workshop, personal methods will bring their own special qualities. With all these factors involved, it is not surprising that people with unlike temperaments, abilities and idiosyncrasies produce extremely varied results.

Glazes and glaze materials are supplied in the form of finely ground powder. They are insoluble in water, in which they are mixed for use. The thickness of the mixture will vary according to the pot (whether it is to be thinly or thickly coated), the glaze, and the potter. A factor which has to be taken into consideration is the biscuit's capacity for absorption. Generally the firing of biscuit is regular and consistent, but variations can occur. With experience the hardness or softness of biscuit can be sensed by a touch of the hand or tested on the tongue. Soft- or low-fired biscuit is more absorbent than hard and a thicker layer of glaze will form. Adjustment is made either by thinning the glaze or damping the pot.

Having prepared the glaze to the right density (see page 60), it is essential to stir it frequently. Failure to do so will mean that the suspended particles will gradually settle to the bottom, and the glaze mixture will be thin at the top and thick lower down. When a glaze has been standing for some time, the particles settle completely with clear water at the top. It is a useful precaution before stirring to remove this water and adjust with fresh water afterwards if necessary. Removing the top water also removes any scummy foreign matter which has found its way in. Stirring should be thorough, with a brush, not a stick.

The application of the glaze is a simple but skilled process, requiring practice, and should be done without hesitation or haste. There are a variety of ways of holding pieces for glazing. The grip must be such that the pot is evenly and completely coated, with as little interference from the fingers as possible, thus needing little or no retouching. The insides of pots arc usually swilled out first, and the outsides covered by dipping or pouring. The pot is often held by its foot when the outside is being treated and this fact should be considered when designing the feature.

Retouching is often unavoidable and the repair of the glazing should be neat and thorough since nothing finally spoils work more than a patchy glaze. It is best done when the glaze has almost dried. At this point it becomes absorbent again and will take more glaze from a small brush. The pot can also be redipped when almost dry, for extra thickness or double glazing. When the glaze is still wet, redipping is ineffective since none will take; and when it is completely dry the first coat is liable to swell suddenly and blister. The glaze coat should be carefully examined for flaws, such as pinholes, bubbles, or cracks appearing especially in thick coats. These and any retouchings should be rubbed and smoothed over gently with a finger; otherwise, instead of fusing together, they will be liable to open and crawl, leaving gaps in the glaze.

In craft pottery, it is the practice to leave the foot of a pot unglazed. This makes for neatness in the glazing, decorative contrast, and ease of handling in the glaze dipping and later in the packing of the kiln. Glazing the foot would necessitate the use of a porcelain spur or support to prevent it sticking to the shelf in the kiln. This not only takes up precious space and needs more care in kiln

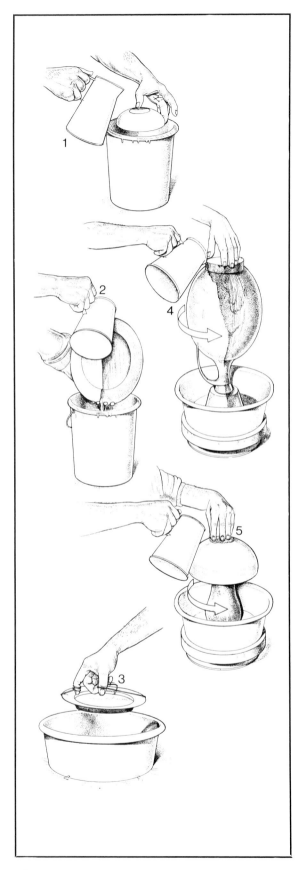

packing, but also the jagged glaze points left by the spur would need grinding and polishing. In stoneware firing, spurs are inadvisable for another reason: clay softens at a high temperature and would distort over a small support. Since the pot has been glazed on the inside, there should be no likelihood of an earthenware piece leaking. The amount of foot left unglazed depends on the type of glaze. Thick and easily melting ones will need more clearance than thin hard glazes, to allow for a tendency to flow downwards.

Finally, before passing work for glost packing, feet must be thoroughly checked for any trace of glaze, which would cause sticking, spoiling both pot and kiln shelf. Glaze on the foot should be removed with a scraper or an old toothbrush and sponge and water. In the glazing of many pieces of the same design, wax resist painted on the feet will save much time; the technique can of course be used on any piece.

Spraying is a very useful way of applying thin even coats, especially over delicate under-glaze painting, which is liable to be disturbed by pouring or dipping. Care must be taken in handling sprayed glazes, the granular texture being easily damaged.

Application of glazes

When pieces can be held by the foot, the pouring of the glaze, first inside and then over the outside of a pot, is simple and straightforward. When this is not possible, other ways must be found to make the glazing efficient.

1 How to hold a pot or bowl at the lip and the shallow foot-rim; this requires a slight retouching of the lip.

2 Glazing a plate or shallow dish. It is balanced almost vertically on three fingertips and steadied against the thumb (behind), while the glaze is flooded on from the right edge, along the top to the other edge. The same technique can be used for the back, or it can be glazed as shown in No. 1.

3 This is an alternative way to glaze a plate; it is the industrial method. Wire claws are made to fit thumb and fingers. The foot can be wax resisted.

4 The glazing of a large pot too big or heavy to be gripped. It rests on a pot inside a bowl which is placed on a banding wheel, and it is steadied as it is turned.

5 The same technique for a large bowl. Already rinsed inside with glaze which has been allowed to become firm, it rests on a pot inside a bowl on the banding wheel.

Glaze recipes

Glazes for raku, earthenware, and stoneware are available from suppliers, ready to use. Below are some typical stoneware glaze recipes which lend themselves to experiment with colouring oxides, firing between 1230°C and 1300°C. All glaze and colour effects are the result of trial and error, and the best way of finding out about them is to test at different temperatures every possible ceramic material, first alone and then in all combinations. This should be done accurately in dry-weight measures (see glaze making on page 60), except in the case of single materials. A complete record is essential, and results must be carefully observed. Tests should be carried out on tiles, made from bodies in use and marked off in 1-inch squares, one square per test.

The kiln packed with glost ware, after a firing, showing how different sizes of shelf prop can be used to suit the work in progress.

Ingredients	Glazes							
	Shiny		*Matte*				*Dry*	
	T1	*B1*	*B2*	*T2*	*R3*★	*T3*★	*T4*	*B4*
Whiting	18	13	20	18	4	20	36	17
Flint	16	8	10	13	–	–	–	15
Feldspar	35	72	48	28	49	–	53	42
Cornish stone	25	–	–	13	–	30	–	–
China clay	6	7	22	28	25	30	11	25
Dolomite	–	–	–	–	22	20	–	–

★dolomite glazes

(with acknowledgments to Dora Billington *B* and Daniel Rhodes *R*)

Glost packing and firing

All unfired glazes are very easily damaged by careless handling. The most vulnerable parts are the lip and the handles; these should therefore not be used or even touched. The foot, being strong and unglazed, is the obvious part by which to hold a pot, otherwise it can be held under its widest place. Experience and practice yet again will develop sense in this matter.

As in all packing, the object is to distribute the pieces evenly but, unlike the packing of biscuit, the pieces must obviously not touch each other. There should be in glost packing a clearance of about half an inch in tall pieces, which may lean slightly, and not less than a quarter of an inch for small pieces.

To prevent plucking, sticking from a runny glaze, or contact with glaze at the foot, kiln shelves are coated with some refractory material such as placing-sand, calcined alumina, or a wash of flint. Being loose, sand and alumina should be spread carefully to avoid overspill onto work below, but with both there is the advantage that kiln shelves can be reversed when glaze spotted or slightly bent. Being washed on, flint is more difficult to remove, and if a shelf is turned over the flint is very liable to flake off onto work below. Alumina is expensive but with skilful glazing very little is needed and it can be used again and again. Packing proceeds otherwise as in biscuit, using props and shelves to place the work. Attention should be paid in the same way to the pyro-couple or the placing of cones. The key note in glost packing is scrupulous care since all work is finished at this firing for good or ill.

Glost firing proceeds more quickly than biscuit. The moisture from glazes is released more quickly and easily, without the same risk as with biscuit. After an initial drying out, the heat can be increased at short intervals until it is full on. Much depends on the size of the kiln, but large pieces should be heated more slowly. If raw pieces are included, the firing must of course be treated as for biscuit.

When the work has reached its maturing temperature, the kiln is switched off and allowed to cool naturally, all openings – the spy holes, air vents and chimneys – are closed so that no cold air can enter and cause cracking in the work. Cooling should continue until work can be removed with a bare hand. Air vents and chimney dampers should not be opened prematurely, and nor should the door. Sometimes the maturing of glazes needs a soaking period at the end, when the temperature is held or allowed to drop very slowly before finally switching off and closing down. This must be decided by experience.

Design

Design is concerned with deciding exactly what a thing one is to make will be like. Three factors are involved: an idea, a material to make it in, and the method of making. In ceramics, for instance, the idea may be of a teapot or of an arrangement of bulges, hollows, colours, and textures. The material could be red clay, and the method throwing or modelling, or both.

The teapot is useful, whereas the other object is meant to intrigue and captivate the senses of sight and of touch. With the teapot the designer is limited by three factors – its efficiency, the nature of clay, and the effects of throwing. But with the other object, only clay and its use have their say; the designer is free otherwise to make anything he fancies. Each case can be judged only by the finished article: the teapot by the way it provides tea, the other by the feelings it awakens. The teapot may also have qualities which repel or attract but these in no way affect its function as a teapot, although they may determine whether one would buy it or not.

In the development of the pot, there has been an underlying and inescapable logic, springing from its function, the nature of clay, and the turning of the wheel, and this extends even into pieces which are not purely functional, but which have intangible mysterious qualities. The design of useful pots has continued for centuries with little or no fundamental changes or startling innovation in function. A pot is primarily a container, the belly dominant and rounded. The foot, throat, mouth, spout, handle or lid extend its function but without threatening the belly's dominance; if they did, the effect would be ludicrous or at best comic. As in human forms there is considerable latitude. But a pot should have balance and unity, look all of a piece.

This seems to leave only the problem of how a useful pot is 'dressed up', which of course begs the question 'should it be decorated?'. The human imagination has always found the surface of a pot irresistible, but forms can be highly satisfying in line and proportion and need nothing more. Yet pottery, it has been said, embraces sculpture and painting: bare forms are beautiful, whereas dress intrigues and disturbs. It is a question of emphasis, and the choice must always be a personal one.

The arrangements of lines, shapes, textures, and colours and their character should grow naturally from the profiles, sections, planes, and personality of the ceramic form, whether these lines represent fish, flowers, females or free forms. Good decoration should enhance form, not disguise its shortcomings. It should be secondary only in the sense that it succeeds form.

Some ceramic forms are designed purely as vehicles for graphic expression, and here there are no limits other than those of graphic design itself and of ceramic materials. The approach is that of the painter, but as the materials are ceramic there would be no purpose in using them if their natural qualities were not evident. In this, as in the making of free ceramic forms, there are no restrictions to the creative designer's complete enjoyment of the qualities of ceramic materials and a sincere imaginative use of them.

By practice a craftsman can gain the knowledge and skill necessary to make good pots. But for those more indefinable attributes, beauty of proportion, line and vitality, some extra sensitivity is required. This can be developed only by endlessly looking at and using sources where these qualities may be found, in the past or in nature. There is no doubt that the simplest pot made by a primitive potter has some dynamic quality. There is also no doubt that now and again some potter with an intuitive gift will go further and transcend what is merely useful.

Workshop practice

Introduction

Cleanliness and order are of paramount importance in the running of a pottery workshop. With so many different stages and processes involved in the making of a pot, the chances of accidental contamination are many. Dirt must be eliminated since in the firing it can ruin work which has taken days of careful preparation. But so must unwanted ceramic materials left carelessly lying around, because they can be absorbed into body or glaze and cause blemishes.

The conditions of space in workshops may vary considerably. In some favourable cases a room is available for each process whereas in others, unfortunately, an instructor may be unable to pack a kiln without falling over a student sticking a handle on a pot. But, whatever space there may be, areas of work should be clearly defined and strictly adhered to. At the very least this should mean a breakdown into the three basic processes: the use of clay in the making and decorating of pots, glazing and the use of colours, and lastly firing and everything associated with the kiln. The kiln is the focal point of the workshop.

All materials and moveable items of equipment should be allocated a permanent place, to which they should be returned immediately after use, and useable waste materials should be properly disposed of.

If proper preparation is an essential part of sound craftsmanship and good work, thorough cleaning up is equally important, and a job should not be considered complete until it has been done. All this sounds obvious but it cannot be over-emphasized since laxity or carelessness can become habitual. These principles should be maintained not only with other people in mind, but in each individual's personal interest as an integral part of good craftsmanship.

The notebook

This should really be a pottery student's first piece of equipment. It takes years to become familiar with ceramic materials and processes, and trusting to one's memory during technical instruction is unwise. The use of a ready-to-hand notebook is essential if progress is to be made and time is not to be needlessly wasted for both student and teacher in repeat instruction.

Ideally there should be two notebooks, both strong and thick enough to survive continual use over several years in the conditions of a busy workshop. The first should be for factual information, gathered during instruction or demonstration, or from any other source. The other notebook, of plain paper, should be for practical working notes, with both descriptions and sketches detailing personal experiments and results as they occur and ideas for design, as well as a record of work done. Good ideas can be very fleeting, easily forgotten and lost. A brief note or drawing is enough to refresh the memory.

Every pottery student should also have a sketch book. Indeed no art student would feel complete without one. The development of visual awareness is essential to anyone concerned with art and crafts, and drawing must become as natural an occupation as writing. No opportunity should be missed of studying and drawing literally anything which may add to this awareness and so feed the imagination.

Although a design idea seems at times to come out of the blue, it is always the result of a slow growth and there must be knowledge for it to germinate. The more knowledge, the more the idea will develop. And just as the fleeting idea needs pinning down, so does the rare glimpse of something compelling seen in nature, in everyday life, or in a museum.

The preparation of glazes and slips

All recipes in pottery are measured by dry weight. In glazes and decorative slips, the amount of water in which they are mixed can vary so as to give different thicknesses. In casting slip, however, the volume of water is precise and requires proper and careful measuring. Amounts in recipes should be measured as percentages, rather than weights, so that they can be easily compared with each other. The unit of weight used depends on the size of the batch required. For experimental purposes 100 grammes carefully weighed on a delicate balance is adequate, but for a working batch of about half a bucket 100 ounces would be required. It is essential that all materials are dry when supplied and kept dry. Any which are damp will obviously upset the recipe.

Preparation consists of accurately weighing the ingredients, soaking them thoroughly in water and sieving the whole batch without loss. Ceramic materials are supplied finely ground but may become lumpy. Regrinding is not necessary, but the smaller the lumps, the quicker the soaking and easier the sieving. When clay is one of the ingredients, enough time should be allowed for it to disintegrate, otherwise stirring will result in lumps difficult to sieve.

Except with casting slip, plenty of water can be used to brush the mixture through the sieve. This, plus the thorough rinsing of bowl, brush, and sieve, ensures that there is no loss, a job done not for economy but because variation of the recipe through loss can effect the result.

Sieves vary according to mesh size, which is measured by the number of holes in a linear inch. For most purposes, 60 to 100 are adequate, 80 being most generally used; individual practice may vary, some glazes needing to be coarser than others and certain colours requiring a very fine sieving.

After the sieving, the glaze or slip should be thoroughly stirred to bring any foreign deposit to the surface as scum. This can be removed, along with clear water after the solids have settled, and the thickness of the mixture adjusted.

All containers for glazes and slips should be kept covered to prevent contamination from dust, always a hazard in potteries. They should also be clearly numbered and labelled with the type, firing temperature and a description, if not the recipe of the contents, so that no error can result from wrongful use. It is particularly necessary to distinguish between high- and low-temperature glazes since an error of this kind could prove disastrous.

A potter's tools

That tools are an extension of the hands is nowhere more evident than in the making of things in clay. Found objects such as pebbles, shells and animal ribs not only help the hands, but even initiate techniques. Tools can still be readily improvised from cast-off materials and worn-out objects of all kinds, and they are a great stimulus to imagination and invention, both in making and decoration. Personal tools and care in handling them are essential to good workmanship; indeed tools must be treated as carefully as the hands themselves. Here only basic tools are shown; all can be improvised.

1 Three flat turning tools, cut and filed from hoop iron (mild steel) or stainless steel, which is more expensive but tougher. Strips should be 16 gauge thick, $1\frac{1}{2}-2\frac{1}{2}$ cms wide and 18 cms long; this provides for a blade of at least 4 cms— its shape will vary as required.

2 Two looped turning tools, made from strips of iron such as packing strip, clock spring, or hacksaw blades (made red-hot for bending).

3 Two tools in one: a sponge stick and a throwing gauge. Bamboo serves as a handle, the sponge being bound with a strong rubber-band over a joint, and the gauge finger being a piece of rubber tubing cut obliquely.

4 A throwing tool. This is a longer version of a turning tool, with a long pointed blade.

5 Callipers. These can be improvised from split bamboo.

6 A shoemender's knife, a worn-out kitchen knife, or a ground, sharpened hacksaw blade.

7 Two drills. Pen nibs of various sizes, reversed in the holder, are ideal for making holes. Thin wires or rods make small holes; thick ones tend to split clay walls and leave ragged holes.

8 A thin awl for trimming lips in throwing, cutting clay slices, and piercing. This is easily improvised—simply a needle sheathed in cork.

9 Four kidneys of rubber and steel, the latter being cockscomb toothed.

10 A pair of hardwood sticks slotted at measured intervals and a stranded wire of stainless steel or brass, for cutting clay slices.

11 A hoop, another device for cutting clay slices. This is made from an old bucket handle and taut wire. Wires for wedging, throwing, and general purposes should be of various thicknesses of nylon or terylene, as used for fishline, or of stranded stainless steel or brass. Copper, galvanized iron, iron, or soft metal should not be used because they wear out quickly or corrode.

12 Slip trailers can be improvised from any rubber bulb, such as a bicycle-horn bulb, fitted with a cork and a ball-point ink tube.

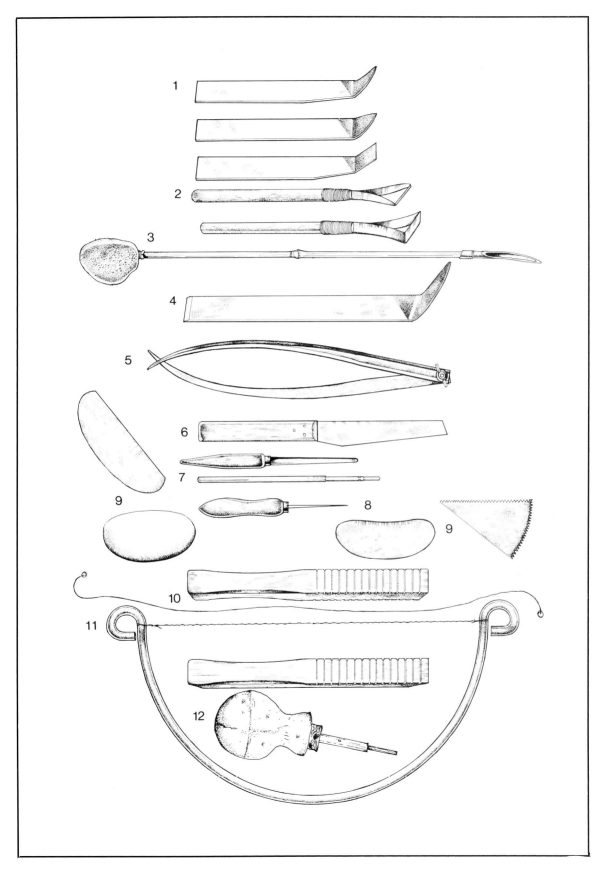

61

Press moulds for shallow dishes

Hollow plaster moulds are made from solid clay models, shaped to the inside section of the dish. There must be no undercut, or turning in at the lip, which would prevent easy release of the dish from the mould. Shapes which are circular in plan are made with plastic clay directly on the wheel-head or a circular bat. Other regular and irregular forms will need to be modelled accurately by eye or by the use of a template, on stiff clay. They are best done on a plaster bat, using a template to shape the clay model. The bat should be about half an inch thick and cut or moulded exactly to the plan of the dish. To make a bat, a clay wall, carefully enclosing the plan drawn on a flat surface, serves as the mould into which plaster is poured and sets level. This bat is a guide for the template as it is moved round to shape the clay model. The template can be cut from stiff card, and an allowance should be made for the height of the bat; the bat itself should first be covered with thin paper so that the model can be easily removed onto a larger board ready for moulding. Both in the modelling and later in the moulding process the work is easier and more efficient if it is carried out on a turntable.

Before moulding can begin a wall must be placed round the model to retain the plaster when it is poured over it. With moulds for dishes up to nine inches across this wall must be built about one and a half inches from the model to allow for the thickness of the mould. The space should be proportionally wider for larger dish moulds. With circular ones made on the wheel, this space should be allowed for on the wheel-head and the wall made simply by tying a strip of zinc round the head. For other simple shapes, the zinc is placed upwards of one and a half inches from the model, and sealed with clay, but with irregular ones a strong clay wall is used. It should be high enough to clear the model by two inches since this will be the thickness of the mould in the middle. With a clay wash over the board or the wheel-head to stop the plaster sticking, the model is ready for moulding.

Plaster of Paris is mixed by adding the powder to the water in correct proportions. Too much powder will make a stiff mix which sets quickly without flowing, and too little will make a weak mould. Plaster varies in quality and grade. With potters' plaster, the proportions should be about twenty-five ounces to the pint. Practice and experience are the best guide, not only for this but also for the quantity needed for the job.

The water is put in a bowl or open jug and the powder sifted in evenly by hand so that the water is absorbed without lumps forming. When all the powder is soaked, the water is stirred, working smoothly by hand to prevent air bubbles from forming. Blending continues and after several minutes the mixture begins to thicken; air bubbles which have formed can be surfaced by tapping the bowl. When this thickening or initial setting has definitely begun, the plaster should be poured gently and evenly over the middle of the model while it is turned slowly to allow the plaster to level itself. The final setting and hardening is indicated by the heat generated through the chemical action of water on the plaster. When this is felt, the zinc or clay wall can be removed but the plaster is still soft enough for trimming with a steel scraper or hacksaw blade. Sharp corners should be rounded off because they chip frequently and because a mould will turn easily on the bench when being used for pressing if the bottom face is slightly curved. Cold water on the mould will release it from the wheel or board and the clay model.

It is important to remember that a chemical action takes place in the mixing of plaster and that adding water during the stirring to try to thin too thick a mixture will result in killing the setting and making it useless. Plaster, while being a very useful material in pottery, can be disastrous if particles or pieces get into clay since this causes trouble in firing. Cleaning up should therefore be thorough, and waste plaster should be properly disposed of in the rubbish bin, not in the sink.

Moulds will gradually dry out with use and should not be forcibly heated, otherwise they will soften or crack. They can be easily duplicated from each other. After being washed and lathered several times with a solution of soft soap, a plaster surface develops a greasy film which will not allow fresh plaster to stick. The mould, with the zinc strip tied firmly round it, can then be filled with fresh plaster. When this has set hard, the mould and the plaster cast can be separated, the cast being a copy of the clay model. This in turn needs soap washing before it can be used for making moulds. It can also be used as a convex mould.

Deep or irregular moulds may be difficult to separate from the cast. In this case, the original mould may have to be broken, but the moulds then made from the plaster model are more easily removed. The model should be lightly soap washed each time another mould is made.

Glossary of terms

Ageing (or souring) The improving of clay by long periods of damp storage.
Banding wheel (or whirler) A hand-operated turntable for coiling or decorating pots.
Bat 1. Any tile or board on which work may be done, or placed, such as kiln shelves, for firing, or bats made of wood, asbestos, or plaster, for throwing, modelling, or drying. 2. A slice of clay.
Bat wash A wash of flint over a kiln shelf to prevent any possibility of sticking during glost firing. Dusting with sand or calcined alumina serves the same purpose.
Blistering and bloating. The first is a fault in glazes, the other in bodies, during firing. They are the result of gas or air bubbles produced by impurities or cavities.
Body 1. The prepared material from which any ceramic article is made. 2. The main part of a pot.
Broken colour Colour which is uneven, with variations of its own, or another, colour.
Calcine To change the structure of a material by heat, reducing it to a powder, or dehydrating it.
Chamotte The French word for grog (q.v.).
Chattering The jumping of a turning tool on hard or coarse clay, especially if the tool is blunt, or incorrectly held, with a slow wheel.
Cockscomb A toothed rib or template.
Combined water Molecular water, a chemical constituent of clay, expelled when heated to over 500°C to form biscuit.
Crackle (or crazing) The cracking of a glaze or slip after firing, due to it not fitting the body.
Crank mixture Grog made from kiln furniture.
Cranks Kiln shelves, flat or specially shaped.
Crawling A glaze fault, in which the glaze crinkles in melting, leaving bare areas of pot. It is due either to dirty or dusty biscuit or to a thickly coated glaze cracking as it dries and not closing in the firing.
Dod box A screw-operated box for extruding clay strips through dies for handles.
Drawing The unpacking of a kiln.
Dunting The cracking of pots when cooled too quickly.
Engobe A coating of slip, generally white, to improve the appearance of a dark or coarse clay.
Fat clays Very plastic clays.
Fettling A general cleaning-up of clay pots.

Fireclay A very refractory clay deposit found under coal seams, used for refractory bricks.
Fit The relationship between body and slip or glaze, a good fit being one in which there is minimal discrepancy in shrinkage and thermal expansion and contraction.
Flaking (or scaling) The peeling of slips and glazes from the pot, before or after firing, due to bad fit (q.v.).
Flux 1. A material used to lower the melting point of other ingredients in glazes. 2. Used to assist in the vitrification of stoneware and porcelain bodies.
Frit A fused mixture of certain fluxes with silica to make them insoluble: lead oxide because it is poisonous, and soda and borax because they are soluble in water.
Glost Glaze or glazed, as in glost kiln, glost ware.
Greenware Finished clay work which is not dry.
Grog Crushed and graded firebricks, cranks, or biscuit.
Hard 1. High-temperature firing. 2. High-fired clay or glaze.
Kaolin A white-firing clay originally used in China, similar to china clay.
Kidney A kidney-shaped template of steel or rubber for scraping and pressing.
Kiln bits Small pieces of broken kiln shelf, useful for packing.
Kiln furniture The shelves, cranks, and props used for supporting ware in the kiln.
Lean clays Those which are short or not very plastic.
Leather-hard The state of clay between plastic and dry.
Lustre A metallic quality produced by the reduction of oxides.
Muffle A refractory box inside the kiln, protecting the ware from direct contact with flames. A semi-muffle gives partial protection, being the lower half of the box.
On-glaze Decoration applied on the glaze, usually ceramic colours and enamels.
Opening materials Non-plastic materials, such as sand and grog, mixed with clay to lessen the risk of cracking in firing. They also reduce plasticity and shrinkage.
Oxidation Firing with enough oxygen to ensure complete combustion of all carbonaceous matter, either in the fuel or in the clay.
Pinholing The effect made in glazes by tiny bubbles of air which have burst but not healed.

Placing-sand Fine white sand used to bed awkward shapes in biscuit packing, and also, when spread on shelves, to prevent sticking and plucking in glost firing.
Plucking Scars left by spurs on a glazed foot or by the sticking of an unglazed foot during glost firing due to vitrification or traces of glaze.
Primary air Air which mixes with fuel before ignition.
Primary clay Clay found where it was formed.
Pug mill A machine for mixing clay.
Pyrometer and pyrocouple Devices for measuring the temperature of a kiln during firing. The meter outside the kiln registers an electrical impulse generated by heat on the couple inside.
Pyrometric cones Cones of ceramic mixtures composed to fuse and bend at specific temperatures.
Raw Unfired.
Raw glazing The application of glaze to a raw pot.
Reduction Used in high-temperature glost firing. Incomplete combustion produces an atmosphere charged with free carbon, which, by combining with the oxygen in colour oxides, reduces them, and results in colour changes.
Refractory Having a high resistance to heat.
Relief decoration Raised modelled decoration.
Resist A decoration technique in which selected areas of clay, biscuit, or glaze are treated so that they reject the application of slip, colour, or glaze.
Ribs 1. Templates of wood, metal, or slate shaped to produce a required profile in clay. 2. The knuckle marks on a thrown pot.
Saggar 1. A refractory box used for packing work in a large kiln; several are stacked one above another. 2. The muffle of a raku kiln.
Salt glaze A stoneware glaze produced by throwing salt (sodium chloride) onto the kiln fire at the maturing temperature. The salt volatilizes, filling the kiln, and the sodium, acting as a flux, combines with the clay surface to form a glaze.
Secondary air Air which assists combustion after the ignition of fuel, mixing with flame and work in the kiln.
Secondary clays Clays which have been eroded and deposited elsewhere by rain and river.
Seger cones Pyrometric cones named after the chemist H.A. Seger (1839–93) who devised them.
Short clay One which is not very plastic.

Slip Clay in a liquid form.
Slip glaze A glaze containing plastic clay, applied to raw clayware.
Slob Lumpy waste from throwing.
Slurry Slip formed in throwing.
Soaking The maturing of biscuit or glaze by maintaining maximum temperature for a period.
Soft 1. Low-temperature firing. 2. Low-fired clay or glaze.
Under-glaze Decoration which is under the glaze.

Vitrification The fusing of a clay body to become impervious like glass.
Weathering The necessary exposure of freshly dug clay to rain and frost, removing soluble impurities and breaking up particles.

Index

Numbers in **bold** refer to captions